Humor in Pharmacy

Cliff Thomas, R. Ph.
The Philosophical Pharmacist

NEMO PUBLISHING COMPANY

1 721 12th Avenue, Belle Fourche, South Dakota 57717-2112

Printed in the United States of America

Cover design and interior art by Marty Grant Two Bulls
Interior design and composition by Top Dog Publishing Co.

ISBN: 0-9666565-0-4

First Edition October 1998

Introduction

Once upon a time, somewhere during the year ???? B.C., two guys named George and Larry came out of their caves after a long winter sleep and built a bonfire by rubbing two Boy Scouts together.

When the fire was going well, they picked a few leaves off a sassfras tree, took a little of the bark, boiled that in water, and became the first pharmacists. That makes pharmacy the world's second oldest profession. I understand the "ladies of the night" beat us by a couple of years.

Sitting around their bonfire and sipping their sassafras tea, they became the first human beings to use medicine to treat a disease, which in their case was spring fever.

While sipping their tea, George turned to Larry and, with a grin on his face, asked, "Why did the chicken cross the road?"

At a complete loss for an answer, Larry replied, "I haven't the faintest idea why the chicken crossed the road."

Chuckling loudly, George responded, "To get to the other side."

Not to be outdone, Larry put his question to George: "Who was that lady I saw you out with the other night?"

George quickly countered, "That was no lady, that was my wife!"

This was the first incident in the history of the profession of pharmacy of pharmacists telling jokes to each other, and it has been going on ever since. Thankfully, the quality of these jokes has improved greatly over the years.

However, if you are not impressed by the jokes of this age, you have to be impressed by the age of these jokes.

As George and Larry continued to sip their sassafras tea, they found it to be very unpleasant to the taste, and it did little for their medical condition — spring fever. In fact, they found their humorous jibes did much more for their human condition. It was they who established that laughter is the best medicine, and that hypothesis continues to this day.

George and Larry continued to bombard each other with jibes and questions, such as, "How come you look so tired this morning?"

Larry responded, "Because I stayed up all night studying for my blood test."

Then, Larry inquired of George: "How do you know your wife really is 28 years old?"

George returned, "I counted the rings under her eyes."

This banter between pharmacists continues to this day but, unfortunately (or fortunately), little of it was recorded. This did, however, become the foundation for *Humor in Pharmacy.*

Throughout the history of our profession, the banter of humorous exchange between pharmacists continued. Soon, it began to rub off on the pharmacists' customers, and more people got into the act. Pharmacists began to exchange jibes with their customers. This led to the foundation of the expression: Tell it to Your Pharmacist.

Then, as other medical professions developed, it began to rub off on them. This series of events led to the development of humor in the health-care professions, which is also a condition that continues to this day.

It has been my endeavor to record and save some of this pharmacy humor for posterity. People have asked me, "How long did it take you to write this book?"

My answer is, "All my life." And that is as it is.

I have been a pharmacist for more than half a century, and I have been saving humorous material most of those years. I like to think that I have one of the largest collections of humor in America.

My library of humor consists of more than 2,500 volumes on all phases of the subject. I have 1,000 cassette tapes and videos of popular comedians and early comedy radio and TV shows. In addition, I have two three-drawer file cabinets filled with items I have clipped from newspapers, magazines and other publications over the years. Also, a good share of this material was given to me by pharmacist friends, other health-care professionals, and Joe Blow who lives down the street. When I am asked where I got this material, my answer is, "From all over!" And, that is just where it came from.

It would be impossible to acknowledge the sources of most of these items, and some of them actually are original. I am deeply indebted to a lot of people for assistance with this project, not the least of them being George and Larry.

Cliff Thomas, R.Ph.
The Philosophical Pharmacist

Dedication

I would like to dedicate this book to all the pharmacists in America who enjoy a good joke, gag or pun, and love to pass them on. Many of these people have supplied material that is included in this publication, for which I am very thankful.

I would also like to dedicate this labor of love to my lovely wife, Marcine, my companion and best friend for more than 50 years.

Also, I would like to dedicate it to my seven children: Susan, Mary, John, Nancy, Barbara, Sally, and Michael and their spouses; and to my 13 grandchildren: Kelly, Katie, John, Tommy, Jeffery, Jeremy, Jennifer, Elizabeth, Christopher, Sara, David, Megan, and Sammi Jo.

All these folks spent countless hours watching me work at my computer.

A Good Luck Wish for the Grand Opening

For a number of years I have been a compliance officer for our State Board of Pharmacy. It's a seasonal position so I do this on a part time basis. I enjoy this job, because it keeps me in touch with many of my friends in pharmacy and I find the work very interesting.

During the "visiting periods" that follow these inspections, I always try to ask each pharmacist the same question. "What's the funniest thing that has ever happened to you in the practice of pharmacy?" I really hear some dandies, and here's an example:

This community pharmacist had a successful pharmacy and decided it was time to enlarge and move to a new location. He built a new building in a prime location, added new fixtures and moved into the most modern pharmacy in the area.

To celebrate the occasion he held a gala grand opening like his town had never seen before. The store was filled with floral arrangements from his many friends and suppliers. He was appalled, however, when he received from his favorite wholesaler a funeral wreath that bore the inscription: REST IN PEACE.

1

When the sales representative for the wholesaler saw the wreath, he was quite unhappy and complained bitterly to the florist.

After apologizing, the florist said, "What happened to you was very bad, but somewhere a man was buried under a wreath today that said, GOOD LUCK IN YOUR NEW LOCATION!

At the Golden Gate

There are among us those skeptics who seem to think that the only way a pharmacist is going to get to heaven is through the back door. Nothing could be farther from the truth and I can prove it.

Witness this true tale which will bear me out:

Three men advanced to the Golden Gate and faced St. Peter, waiting to be admitted into heaven. St. Peter explained the rules and regulations and then added, "Before I can give you your final admission, I have to ask you some questions. First, I must know how much you earned last year."

The first man said, "I owned my own bank in a small town and I learned about $400,000 last year."

The second man said, "I was a lawyer in a small town and I made about half a million dollars last year."

The third man said, "I made about $8,000 last year."

"Really," said St. Peter, "Where did you have your pharmacy?"

Cliff Thomas

Editor
Rapid City Journal
P.O. Box 450
Rapid City, SD 57709

Dear Editor:

My wife and I enjoy our retirement here in the beautiful Black Hills. Being strongly dependent on our Social Security checks, we appreciate the generosity of the Deadwood casino operators when we experience too much month at the end of the money.

Last week our finances needed a transfusion so we headed for Deadwood. We had heard about the aggressiveness of the Deadwood police department but were pleased to read the mayor's statement that it was more a matter of poor public relations than harassment.

With the construction, we went through Sturgis and noticed we were low on gas. We filled the tank at the junction and I spilled some gas on my arm and it ran down to my elbow. We smelled gas when I got back into the car but we overlooked it.

As we entered the Deadwood city limits my wife lit up a cigarette and my whole arm burst into flame. We were able to extinguish the flame and though I zigzagged all over the road, I regained control without incident.

One of Deadwood's finest observed my driving and pulled me over. I was ticketed for possession of a firearm.

Yours truly:
Cliff Thomas, R.Ph.

A Friend Not in Need Is Not a Friend Indeed

Swenson had a pharmacy in a small town in Wyoming and loved the game of football. He was an ardent Denver Broncos fan, and while he had never attended a game in person, he seldom missed one on TV.

A salesman, who had called on Swenson for several years, knew of his admiration for the Broncos and gave him a ticket to a home game at Mile High Stadium in Denver. Swenson hired a relief pharmacist and attended the game.

Unfortunately, the seat was in the last row in the end zone section and perhaps the worst seat in the stadium.

Swenson had brought his field glasses, and in viewing the stadium he saw an empty seat on the 50-yard line about four rows up. This had to be one of the best seats in the house and it was empty. After a little thought, he decided that if no one was going to use the seat, why couldn't he.

He decided to give it a try, and made his way past the security police and found the seat. As he stood by the seat, he asked the man next to it if anyone was sitting there.

The man assured him that the seat was empty and Swenson slid into it, happy as he could be. He went on to explain to the man that he had a seat in the end zone and saw this empty seat while viewing the crowd through his binoculars. "I can't believe that anyone would have a choice seat like this for a Denver Broncos game and not use it," said Swenson.

"Actually," said the man, "the seat belongs to me. My wife and I have had these seats as long as we have been married. She passed away and this is the first game she has missed in 23 years."

"I'm very sorry to hear that," said Swenson. "But this is one of the best seats in the stadium. Couldn't you find a relative or a good friend to be your guest?"

"No," replied the man, "they're all at the funeral."

A Lesson in Bible History

The Bible history teacher asked the first year class, "Can anyone tell me where Jesus was born?"

No one raised a hand, so she looked at the pharmacist's son and said, "Jerome, can you tell me where Jesus was born?"

In deep thought, Jerome answered, "Was it Pittsburgh?" he asked.

"No, it wasn't Pittsburgh, Jerome, try again."

"Philadelphia?" asked Jerome.

"No, Jerome, it wasn't Philadelphia either," said the teacher. "It was Bethlehem."

"Darn!" said Jerome, "I knew it was somewhere in Pennsylvania."

An Experience With a Professional

This very busy, hard working pharmacist was spending a quiet weekend at home with her family, while her husband was attending an out of town meeting.

A problem developed with her kitchen sink, so she called the plumber to her house. The plumber assessed the situation and told the pharmacist: "I can fix the problem, but before I start I want you to know it's double time on weekends. The fee is $80 per hour!"

"Eighty dollars per hour," she exclaimed, "Why, I'm a pharmacist and that's more than I make!"

"Hey, don't feel bad," said the plumber, "When I was a pharmacist, I didn't make that much either."

America May be the Land of the Free But Not the Debt-Free

Pharmacist Jack Jones had a serious financial problem in his drug store - expanding accounts receivable. His most serious past due account was more than six months past due.

He had sent a series of past due statements and letters requesting payment without success.

Finally he wrote a desperate, pathetic letter and enclosed a picture of his infant daughter. On the back of the snapshot he wrote, "The reason I need the money!"

A week later he received a response in the mail. A picture of a gorgeous woman clothed only in a beautiful mink coat. Scribbled on the back of the photo: "The reason I can't pay!"

A Burglar Always Tries to Live
Within Another Man's Means

A pharmacist in Minneapolis was surprised to find that someone had stolen the battery out of his car while it was parked in front of his house. Stuck to the windshield of his car was a note apologizing for the theft of the battery.

The thief explained that his car battery had gone dead, so he merely borrowed the battery and would return it in a few days.

Sure enough, soon the battery turned up on their door step along with a note thanking them, and two tickets to the Minnesota Vikings football game that weekend. The pharmacist was pleased with the gift of the free tickets and he and his wife eagerly went to the game.

When they returned, they found their home had been ransacked.

A Wise Golfer

If you are shooting in the 90s, you better watch your golf. If you're shooting in the 80s you better watch your business!

You can always spot a pharmaceutical detail man who is playing golf with his boss. He's the fellow who makes a hole in one and says "oops".

Cass, a pharmaceutical service representative, was a pretty fair golfer. He managed to play a couple of times a week in the various towns where he made his calls.

His new district manager made arrangements to travel Cass's territory with him and invited Cass to an afternoon of golf while making their calls.

Attempting to convey to his boss that he was new to the game, Cass teed off first. His drive bounced along the fairway to a distance of about 30 yards. With a frown on his face, Cass turned to his boss and said, "Any advice?"

The boss looked at Cass and said, "Really, I think your ball will go farther if you take the hood off the driver."

A Real Shaggy Dog Story

When pharmacists get together in social situations they like to talk about experiences they have encountered when customers have asked them to recommend products. What's good for this? What's good for that? Pharmacists like to expound on the strange circumstances from which these requests evolved.

I have a pharmacist friend who operated a drug store in a small town of 500 people in the mid-1950s. Main Street was three blocks long, then it started up a very steep hill. At the top of the hill was the cemetery. From his prescription counter my friend could look out the side window and see the cemetery. The funeral home was three doors from the drug store, and in the mid-1950s it still used a horse drawn hearse.

It was about 3 p.m. on a cold February day; the streets were very icy and a funeral was in procession. It passed the drug store and started up this steep hill to the cemetery as my friend watched from his prescription counter.

About three-quarters of the way to the top of the hill, the latch came loose at the back of the hearse and the casket slipped out. It hit the icy street and started sliding down the steep hill, rapidly picking up speed along the way.

It came right down Main Street, very rapidly, hit a lamp post in front of the drug store, did a 90 degree turn, jumped the curb, crashed through the front window of the drug store, slid across the floor and banged up against the prescription counter. As my friend leaned across the prescription counter, the casket bounced back, the lid popped open, a head popped up and the guy said, "Have you got anything at all that will stop this coffin!"

Is that a "shaggy dog" story? Woof! Woof! Woof!

8

A Happy Birthday Message

We participated in an externship program established by the college of pharmacy at South Dakota State University to give students practical pharmacy experience during the summer months. We are located in the beautiful Black Hills of Western South Dakota. In addition to the pharmacy, we owned and operated an apartment complex and were able to offer the students a very comfortable, furnished apartment to occupy during their stay with us. As a result we became a popular place for students to do their externship and we helped train some outstanding students under this program.

We attempted to give these future pharmacists hands-on experience in community pharmacy. Our message was: If you build your business on customer service, being friendly, and always going the extra mile, doing what is best for the customer, the success of your pharmacy is automatic.

Our apartment complex had a number of retired people as tenants and most of them were customers in our pharmacy. One was a special lady who looked much younger than her years and was very proud of it. She spent a lot of money at our cosmetic counter to maintain that appearance and we always considered her our favorite customer. We gave her immediate and very special attention when she came to shop.

It was an extremely hot July afternoon and we were experiencing a record breaking heat wave. A new extern was starting his first day on the job and he had been strongly indoctrinated on the principals under which we operated. He was walking the floor to become acquainted with the layout and the merchandise mix when the front door opened and in came our favorite customer.

It was obvious she was uncomfortable with the heat and as she entered the store she stopped at the cosmetic counter, opened her purse and removed her handkerchief. Seeing our new extern in his white coat, she smiled at him as she wiped her brow and said, "Going to be 104 today!" Our industrious extern returned her smile and said, "HAPPY BIRTHDAY!"

If a Little Knowledge is Dangerous, A Lot of Dangerous People are Wandering Around

If the world becomes any more confused than it is now, don't be surprised to see monkeys tossing peanuts to people.

That's my way of telling you that some mighty strange things happen at the prescription counter. Here's an example:

I was in the dispensing area on what seemed to be a normal day, when a young woman entered the store and headed for the prescription counter. I gave her my big "welcome" smile, and she handed me a prescription. It was for a suspensory for her husband, but it didn't indicate the size.

I said, "The doctor didn't specify what size to dispense, they come small, medium, large, and extra large. Do you know which it should be?"

She raised her eye brow in bewilderment and replied, "I'm not certain, but I do know he wears a fifteen and a half collar."

10

A Dog is the Only Friend
You Can Buy for Money

I always look forward to attending our state pharmacy convention. I have not missed a state convention in 33 years.

One of the big rewards of attendance is the friendships I have made and enjoyed over the years. One of my favorites is my pharmacist friend, George, whom I met many years ago.

George spent several years on the road as a detail man before buying his own pharmacy, so he's a seasoned pharmacist who has been around a long time. One of his most valuable assets is his marvelous sense of humor, and I always look forward to hearing his stories about his experiences.

I cannot vouch for the authenticity of this story, but George says it actually happened. Knowing his strong reputation for honesty, I must believe him. He said the incident happened while he was a detail man working for a major pharmaceutical manufacturer. He was in a pharmacy waiting to speak to the pharmacist as the event unfolds. Here is the story just as he told it to me:

This lady had a little dog, a miniature Schnauzer, that was very friendly and well behaved. The dog developed a hearing problem, so she took him to the vet to have his hearing checked.

After a thorough examination the vet explained that the dog had a heavy growth of hair over his ears and that was the cause of the hearing problem. He proceeded to clip the hair that had grown over the dog's ears, and the hearing returned to normal.

The vet told her he would give her a prescription for a hair remover that she should apply to the area around the dog's ears about once a month to retard the hair growth, and that should take care of the problem. He also advised her that, because of the dog's heavy hair, the depilatory solution would be very strong. She should wear rubber gloves when she applied it.

She stopped at the pharmacy to have the prescription filled, and the pharmacist studied it with deep concern. He realized it was a depilatory, but could see that it was extremely concentrated.

Addressing the patient very professionally, the pharmacist said, "I don't know if you are going to use this on your face, your legs, or under your arms, but you certainly should dilute it about 10 to one."

The patient quickly replied, "Oh no! It's for my Schnauzer!"

In that case," said the pharmacist, "you had better dilute it 20 to 1 and don't ride a bicycle for two weeks!"

All the World Knocks a Knocker

Two pharmacists were attending their state convention and were having a friendly drink in the bar. Both were owners of drug stores in different areas of the state, and as usually happens, the conversation led to business conditions in their area.

"Businesses in our town are really in trouble and my store is having a bad year," said the first pharmacist. "January was a wash out, the December receivables didn't come in. It was a very cold winter and we lost $10,000 in February. In March our losses went to $15,000, and in April, over $20,000 went down the drain."

"Wait a minute," said the second pharmacist. "If you think you've had it bad, let me tell you about us. Last month our only son, 22 years old, came home from college. He told us he was in love -- with another man! What could be worse than that?"

The first pharmacist countered, "JULY!"

A Man Never Knows
Who His Friends Are

The pharmaceutical manufacturer's representative and his sales manager were traveling his country sales territory. It was the middle of the winter, and they were in a remote area when an unannounced snow storm began to arrive.

The salesman knew how intense this weather could become and advised that they find a place where they could ride out the storm. As luck would have it, they spotted a farm house about a mile off the road, so they headed for it.

It turned out that the farm house was owned and occupied by a middle-aged widow lady who lived alone, having lost her husband several years before.

She realized how dangerous these winter storms could be, and invited the men to stay and wait out the storm. However, because the house was small and she was alone, she told them they would have to sleep in the barn. The barn looked comfortable enough, so the two men agreed this was acceptable.

The barn was sturdy but small, and the ground floor was filled with livestock, so they decided to sleep in the hay loft. Due to some leaks in the roof, they selected separate corners of the barn to make their beds. The next day the storm subsided, the widow fixed them an elegant breakfast, and they continued on their way.

About a year later, the salesman called his sales manager and inquired, "Do you recall traveling with me last year and spending the night in the hay loft of that barn when the snow storm hit?"

"Yes," replied the sales manager, "I remember it well, it was a unique experience."

"Tell me," said the salesman, "you didn't happen to get up during the night and visit that old widow at the farm house, did you?"

"Well," said the sales manager, "this embarrasses me very much, but yes, I did."

"When you did this, you didn't happen to tell her that you were me, did you?"

The sales manager confessed. "It was a dirty trick to pull and I'm sorry I did it, but, yes, I did use your name. What can I do to make it right with you?"

"Nothing, nothing at all," said the salesman. She died last month and left me the farm!"

A Pharmacist's Formula
For a Successful Marriage

Pharmacist Minard and his wife operated a very successful pharmacy in their small community for many years. Finally they decided it was time to retire and sold their store to an enterprising young pharmacist.

The Minards loved their small community and decided to remain there in retirement. They traveled to visit children and grandchildren, and spent a few months in the South during the winter, but their community remained their home.

They were celebrating their 65th wedding anniversary and the community turned out in full support to help them celebrate.

The community radio station and the area TV crew showed up to interview them. The question was asked, "To what do you contribute the success of your long marriage?"

Minard replied, "It's a very simple formula. Twice each week we go out for a candle light dinner, some soft music and a little dancing. She goes on Tuesday and I go on Thursday."

A Stitch in Time Saves Nine

The pharmacist's son was in his second year of pharmacy at the university. The father desperately wanted his son to be a pharmacist, but it was costing him an arm and a leg to keep him in school.

The son had about run out of methods to get money out of the old man and it was creating problems with his social life at school.

Finally he hit on a new idea. The son always had a dog at home and both he and his father were very much attached to the dog. Just before the son left for the university the dog died of old age and both of them missed him very much.

The son wrote his father, "I sure miss old Shep, Dad. I have an opportunity to purchase a little puppy. His name is Boomer, and he looks just like Shep. If you would send me a hundred dollars, I could buy him." The father sent the check.

A short time later the son wrote his father again. "I

took Boomer to class with me yesterday, Dad, and my professor was really impressed by him. He said he had never seen such an intelligent dog and for one hundred dollars he would teach the dog to talk. If you would send me a check for a hundred dollars, I will have my professor instruct him." The father sent the check.

In no time the son wrote the father another letter. "Boomer can talk like you wouldn't believe, Dad. The professor gave him an "A" in the speech class. He said that Boomer is even smarter than he originally thought, so for another hundred dollars, he could teach him to read. If you would send me a check for a hundred dollars, I will sign Boomer up for the course." The father sent the check.

The end of the semester was coming up and the son was making plans to come home for Christmas. The father wrote his son, "When you come home next week, son, be sure to bring Boomer with you. I'm anxious to meet him."

When the son arrived home he and his father exchanged pleasantries, then the father asked, "Where's Boomer?"

The son looked very sad and said, "He's dead, Dad, I killed him."

"Why in the world would you do that?."

"Well, I'll tell you Dad," said the son. "Boomer and I were in the apartment getting ready to come home. I was in the bathroom shaving with that old straight edge razor that you gave me that used to belong to grandpa. Boomer was sitting in his easy chair reading the newspaper. He turned to me and said, 'I wonder if the old man is still entertaining the hired girl.'"

"What did you do, son?"

"I cut his throat, Dad."

"Good for you, son!"

Apple Juice

I do some hours as a relief pharmacist at an area hospital, filling in for vacations and sick leaves, and during busy periods. One of the charge nurses is a seasoned old warrior, who runs her shift like a first sergeant.

An old cowboy was admitted to the hospital and he had no desire to be there. She kept a tight rein on him and he wasn't happy.

She was making her morning rounds and entered the cowboy's room. When she took his temperature, she said, "We're a little warm this morning, aren't we?" When she took his blood pressure, she said, "Our pressure is up a little this morning, isn't it?" When she took his pulse, she said, "Our rate is a little fast this morning, isn't it?"

As he was being served his breakfast, she came in with a specimen bottle and said she would pick it up after he finished his breakfast. On his breakfast tray was a glass of apple juice. He hated apple juice so he poured it into the specimen bottle.

When she picked up the specimen bottle, she held it up to the light and said, "We're a little cloudy this morning, aren't we?"

He said, "We are? Let me take a look at it." She handed the bottle to him and he held it up to the light and answered, "You're right, it's cloudy." With that he tipped up the bottle and drank down the apple juice, looked at her, smiled and said, "We'll run it through one more time!"

All He Wants for Christmas is a Five-Pound Box of Money, Gift-Wrapped

It was getting close to Christmas and Grady, the pharmacy tech, had directed a lot of business to a friendly pharmaceutical salesman named Brewster, who worked on commission.

Brewster wanted to show his appreciation to Grady for all the business he had given him and offered him a gift of a TV set.

Grady thanked the salesman very much for the kindness and thoughtfulness of offering him a gift. However, he went on to explain that there is a company policy that would not allow him to accept a gift from a salesman the company does business with.

In view of the company policy, the salesman inquired, "How would it be if I offered to sell you the TV set for $5?"

Grady told the salesman, "I don't know about that, but I will ask the boss."

Grady approached his boss with the offer of the TV set and asked if it would be proper for him to purchase it for $5.

The pharmacist owner told the pharmacy tech, "Tell that salesman that for $5, we'll take two TV sets."

The Open Hand Holds More Friends Than the Closed Fist

Even the man who can't pay his debts has something to be thankful for - he can be glad he isn't one of his creditors.

Mulvaney's Pharmacy wasn't doing very well and he had a lot of money problems. On top of that, he had developed a heart condition, so his doctor advised him to consider retirement. He knew he couldn't afford to retire but he knew he should follow her advice.

Mulvaney was a religious man and decided that the shortest road to a financially successful retirement would be to win the state lottery. Twice every week he said a short prayer and purchased $20 worth of lottery tickets.

One day while Mulvaney was at the drug store, his wife received a phone call saying her husband had won $5 million in the state lottery. While she was thrilled with the message, she realized that with the condition of Mulvaney's heart the news could be a shock. To properly prepare him for the news, she asked the parish priest to deliver the message.

The priest went to the drug store, told Mulvaney he had stopped in for a friendly visit, and invited him to join him for a cup of coffee.

After an exchange of friendly conversation, the priest set down his coffee cup and said to Mulvaney, "Let's just suppose that you had won a lot of money. How would it affect you? What would you do?"

"Well," said Mulvaney, "I've always been a religious man, and I have always admired and respected you, Father. If I won a lot of money, I would be thankful to the Lord for my good fortune. I would give half of it to you for our church."

The priest dropped dead!

19

A Case of Mistaken Identity

Cathcart was a hard working community pharmacist who was very popular in his home area and he was going through the chairs of his state pharmacists association. His secret ambition was to become an officer in his national pharmacists association, so he never missed an opportunity to be highly visible at any pharmacy gathering.

His wife was his working partner in his corner drugstore and she was an important factor in the success of that venture. Since it was a small business she always stayed home to look after the store while Cathcart attended the meetings and conventions. He continuously assured her, however, that she wasn't missing anything because  these events were nothing but work, work, work.

He was getting ready to attend a national pharmacy convention and at the last minute received a notice that the presidents ball would be a masquerade ball with a fine prize for the best costume. Cathcart told his wife about the costume ball and asked her to rent him an appropriate costume. She found an elaborate pirate costume, packed it with his luggage and sent him on his way.

The next day she got to wondering about her husband's activities at these conventions and since this one was at a nearby city, she decided to check up on him. She returned to the costume shop, rented a costume for herself and took off for the convention. She arrived just before the masquerade ball, registered anonymously, changed into her costume, and went off to the ball to check up on her husband.

It was her first convention so she knew no one, but sure enough, there was the pirate, out on the dance floor, the most conspicuous man at the ball. He was dancing with every young thing he could find, showing some fancy steps and having a great time. It was obvious that he was looking for some fun.

Determined to teach him a lesson, she sidled up to him on the dance floor, gave him a strong come-on, and soon she had all of his attention.

After a few drinks and a lot of exotic dancing, he took a much-needed break. She realized it was nearing midnight and time for the unmasking, so she slipped out of the ballroom.

Having laid the groundwork for her master plan, she left the ball before the midnight unmasking and drove back to their home to wait for his return.

A couple of days later Cathcart arrived home from the convention and over morning coffee his wife inquired, "How was the convention?"

"It was a typical convention, you know how they are, work, work, work, nothing but work," he said.

"How was the costume ball?" she asked.

"Well, to tell you the truth, I didn't get there," he replied. "Late in the afternoon I got the worst case of stomach flu I've ever had. I went to bed and missed it all.

"But, I loaned that pirate costume to Charlie and he had a wonderful time, and then he won the grand prize."

The Secret of Successful Treatment Is Getting Started

Old Doctor Crawford had practiced medicine in a rural area for 40 years. It was not beyond him to make a house call, even if it was a few miles from town.

When Effington, one of his long-time patients, called the doctor to come out and see his wife, he responded at once.

When he arrived at the farm house, he was ushered into the sickroom and left with the patient. A few minutes later, the doctor stuck his head out the door and asked the husband for a screwdriver. Minutes later, he followed with a request, "Have you got a hammer?" The husband was puzzled but he got the doctor a hammer. Five minutes later, the doctor came out of the room and asked for a hacksaw.

Effington was beside himself. "Doctor, what are you doing to my wife?," he demanded.

"It's not your wife," replied the doctor. "I'm trying to open my bag!"

Do it Tomorrow.
You Have Made Enough Mistakes Today

The new employee at the wholesale drug company stood before the paper shredder looking confused. A passing secretary realized this was a new employee, so she stopped to inquire, "Do you need some help?"

"Yes," replied the new employee, "How does this thing work?"

"It's easy," said the secretary, as she took the report from the new employees hand and fed it into the shredder.

Even more puzzled, the new employee asked, "Thanks, but where do the copies come out?"

It's Time to Retire

Since a tired and worn out old pharmacist had operated his corner drug store for 40 years, he and his wife decided it was time to sell out and retire. They advertised their pharmacy for sale in a leading pharmacy publication.

In no time at all a young, ambitious pharmacist answered the ad, liked what he saw and purchased the drug store. The tired old pharmacist and his wife retired and moved to the suburbs.

There was some crime in their new location, so they decided they should have a watchdog to guard the house when they were away. They went to the kennel and bought the largest dog they could find.

Not long afterward, burglars broke into the house. Their watch dog slept through the break-in, and the burglars were not disturbed in the least.

The old pharmacist was extremely upset and went to the kennel to complain. The kennel manager explained, "What you need now is a little dog to wake up the big dog!"

It's Still the Same Old Story

When it comes to pharmacy stories, there are a lot of old groaners out there. Pharmacists were telling some of these stories to each other back in the days of snow globes and the bubonic plague. However, they have stood the test of time and are still kicking around, so I feel it is proper to pass them on. You may not be impressed by stories of this age but you should be impressed by the age of these stories!

A timid little gentleman entered the pharmacy and approached the pharmacist with a question, "Could you possibly fix a dose of castor oil so it won't be tasted?"

"Sure," said the pharmacist. "I can do that. Here is a ticket for a free root beer. Step over to our soda fountain and enjoy it. I'll be with you shortly."

The gentleman willingly accepted the invitation and headed for the soda fountain.

The pharmacist returned to him shortly and said, "How did you like the root beer?" The gentleman said he enjoyed the root beer and thanked the pharmacist profusely.

"Well," said the pharmacist, "The castor oil was in it and you didn't even taste it."

The timid little man looked at the pharmacist in amazement and said, "It was my wife who wanted the castor oil."

It Takes a Lot of Suits to Keep
A Lawyer Well-Dressed

Hollowell thinks that playing golf is a lot like being in the drug business. You drive hard to get in the green and then wind up in the hole.

It was his afternoon off, and he was on the third hole of his local course. He hooked his tee shot and saw it disappear over the hill in the direction of the next fairway. He started walking toward the direction of his lie, and when he reached the crest of the hill he saw a man lying on the ground, kicking his feet and moaning. It was obvious he was in a lot of pain.

As Hollowell approached, the injured man yelled, "I'm a lawyer, and this is going to cost you $5,000."

"I'm terribly sorry this happened," said Hollowell, "but I did yell, 'Fore!'"

"I'll take it!," the lawyer said.

People Would be in Better Health
If They Didn't Get Sick so Much

The salesman was making his first call at our drug store, and I immediately saw that he looked ill. I was concerned about his condition and I asked him if he felt well.

"Not really," he said. "In fact, I feel terrible. I have hardening of the arteries, arthritis, glaucoma, high blood pressure, bronchitis, and dizziness."

I told him that I was very sorry to hear of his condition and I asked, "What have you been doing?"

"I'm doing the same thing I've been doing for the last 20 years," he said, "I'm selling health foods."

It's Not Always Easy to Save a Buck

Swenson was a very personable pharmacist. He was kind to everyone and gave good service. Many people stopped in to ask his advice, and some just to visit.

One old gal who had a reputation for being close with a dollar, entered the pharmacy to ask Swenson for some advice. She had a medical problem and wanted him to recommend a physician.

Swenson suggested the physician he thought would do her the most good, but cautioned, "She's very busy and very expensive. She charges $250 for the first visit and $100 for each visit after that. But, she's the one to see for the problem you have."

With the idea of saving some money, she greeted the doctor by saying, "I'm back again!"

The doctor examined her and said, "You've got the same thing you had last time. Just continue the treatment I prescribed for you on your last visit."

Discretion: The Better Part of Valor

The Werners were ushered into the dentist's office, and Mr. Werner made it clear that he was in a big hurry. "No fancy footwork, Doc," he said. "No gas, no needles, none of that malarkey. Just pull the tooth and get it over with."

The dentist was astonished and replied, "I'm really impressed with your bravery. I wish I had more patients like you; I could save a lot of time. Now, which tooth is the one that is giving you the problem?"

Werner turned to his wife and said, "Open wide, dear, and show him the tooth."

He Was Beginning to See the Light

The doctor was giving this 85-year-old retired pharmacist his annual physical examination.

The doctor said, "You are really doing quite well but, have you told me everything?"

"Well," said the pharmacist, "I'm really feeling great, and God is looking after me."

"What do you mean by that?," inquired the doctor.

"Every time I get up during the night to go to the bathroom, the Lord turns on the light for me. It doesn't matter if I get up once or 10 times during the night, the Lord always turns on the light for me."

When the examination was finished, the doctor told the pharmacist's wife he would like to visit with her about her husband.

"What did you find wrong, doctor?," asked the wife.

"Nothing I can find physically, but mentally, I think your husband is developing some problems. He tells me that every time he gets up to go to the bathroom during the night, the Lord turns the light on for him."

"Oh, my goodness!," exclaimed the wife. "He's been going in my refrigerator again!"

Can You Top This?

Dr. Culbertson was a pharmacy doctor and the chief pharmacist at a regional hospital pharmacy. The pharmacy served the 200-bed hospital and a 250-bed extended care facility. There was plenty to keep the staff of 12 pharmacists and 15 pharmacy technicians busy. The pace was usually hectic.

Near the hospital was Dewey's Bar, which was a frequent stopping-off place for hospital personnel.

Dewey, the genial bartender, was a renowned authority on world events, personal finance, the total sports picture and affairs of love and marriage.

He was not beyond adding his personal thoughts on the latest developments in the field of heath care. An avid reader, Dewey kept current on events in this field and could knowledgeably discuss them with the health care professionals who visited his establishment.

Our pharmacist friend, Dr. Culbertson, was a frequent patron.

Promptly at 5:15 p.m. each Friday, Dr. Culbertson would come through the door for his favorite weekly toddy. These visits never failed to happen, and Dewey looked forward to them, so much so that he always had the pharmacist's drink ready and waiting.

Dr. Culbertson's specialty was a walnut and rum drink served over shaved ice, which Dewey prepared with great flourish.

One Friday afternoon, Dewey was frantic to find he had run out of walnuts. But, being a great improviser, he substituted another nut.

Dr. Culbertson came in as usual, tested the drink and looked at the bartender in wonder and asked, "Is this a walnut daiquiri, Dewey?"

Dewey smiled and replied, "No, it's a hickory daiquiri, Doc!"

Grandparents Are People Who Come to the House, Spoil the Children, and Then Go Home

My 5-year-old grandson came for a visit, and the highlight of his trip was to spend a day with Grandpa at the drug store. Mondays are hectic in the pharmacy, and to add to the confusion, there was a highway construction project in front of the drug store.

My grandson was fascinated with the road construction activity, so I set up a chair in the front window so he could have a prime viewing location. He spent most of the day in the chair watching, deeply interested in the road building activity.

At the end of the day, we were returning home and stopped at the supermarket to fill a grocery order as Grandma had instructed us to do. We were preceded in the checkout line by an extremely large woman with a pager attached to her belt.

As we awaited our turn, the pager sounded with a "BEEP, BEEP, BEEP." My grandson threw his hands in the air and screamed, "Look out, Grandpa, she's going to back up!"

Choose the Generic Equivalent

I was behind my prescription counter; it was a normal day and things were moving right along.

A distinguished looking gentleman approached the counter and handed me a prescription for a blood pressure medicine.

He said he had just moved to the area and was new to our pharmacy, so I had him fill out a patient profile questionaire.

As I entered the information into my computer, I noted he had not taken this medicine before, so I began discussing the product with him, beginning the patient counseling procedure.

I told him how to take the medicine and some side effects he might experience. I explained to him that the medicine prescribed was available as the brand name product or I could supply the generic equivalent. I added that neither the brand product nor the generic equivalent would be expensive, but the generic equivalent would be less expensive. We discussed the pros and cons of brand names vs. generic, and he decided he would take the brand name product.

I led him to the cash register. The total price came to $17.45, but I hit the wrong key and the total came up as $1745.00. We both saw this total and he looked at me, raised his eyebrows and said, "I wish I had taken the generic brand!"

Some Cannibals Take Their Missionaries With a Grain of Salt

Spencer sold his drug store and retired to the life of leisure. He soon found that retirement wasn't for him. Being a religious man, he decided to volunteer for a missionary assignment in Africa.

He had no more than arrived when he was captured by cannibals. Each day they would poke him with spears and use his blood to wash down their food.

Finally, Spencer demanded to speak to the chief. "I came over here to help you people," he told the chief. "I want to be friendly with you and help you go to heaven. This has turned out to be a one-sided deal. I want you to know that I am darn tired of getting stuck for all the drinks!"

His Friends Call It Madness
But He Calls it Golf

Volker owned the village pharmacy and was an ardent golfer. Every Wednesday during the season he and his friend Biggs, a pharmaceutical sales representative, played 18 holes without fail. They had been doing this for many years and seldom missed a date.

One day Volker was late returning home, and as darkness fell his wife began to worry. Dinner time passed, and she was sure there was a problem. Finally, she heard the garage door open and she went out to meet him. "What delayed you," she inquired, "I've been worried about you!"

"It was a bad day," said Volker. "We were playing 18 holes, and Biggs had a heart attack on the third hole."

"That's terrible," said his wife, "what did you do?"

"It was a long day," said Volker. "From then on it was hit the ball, drag Biggs, hit the ball, drag Biggs. ..."

I Haven't Been Sleeping Well

An elderly lady approached my prescription counter and asked if I could recommend a product to help her with a problem. She said she hadn't been sleeping well.

I discussed the various reasons why people have this problem and asked if the problem happens in the early evening or later in the night.

"Really," she said, "I sleep good nights, and I sleep pretty good mornings, but afternoons I just seem to twist and turn!"

Letter to an Advice Columnist

Dear Miss Advice:

I have a serious personal problem and I have to make a very important decision. I hope you will be able to give me some desperately needed advice.

I have two brothers, one is a pharmaceutical service representative, and the other is a convicted serial killer.

My father died in the electric chair at the state penitentiary, and my mother was convicted of dealing illegal drugs. My younger sister works in a house of prostitution, and the older one is serving a life sentence for murdering two of her husbands. My only uncle swindled over a million dollars from the bank he worked for.

I have just met a wonderful girl. I love her very much and she has told me she is in love with me. I want to ask her to marry me but this is my problem: Do you think I should tell this girl about my brother who is a pharmaceutical service representative?

Yours very truly,

A Concerned Pharmacy Tech

A Pharmacist's Accounts Receivable Problem

Nothing will send a retail pharmacist to the poor house faster than letting his accounts receivable get out of hand.

My friend Bob, the pharmacist, was in such a situation.

He had made himself a popular person with his liberal charge account policy, however, his cash flow was stagnant and his banker was unhappy. Realizing he had a serious problem, he called in a credit management consultant.

The consultant made a study of the problem and set up an age analysis system for the pharmacy's accounts receivable.

Then he suggested that Bob write little demanding

notes on the bottom of the statements when they became 60 or more days past due.

At the end of the month, Bob prepared his statements.

On the bottom of one of the past due statements he wrote in very large letters: "THIS BILL IS ONE YEAR OLD TODAY!"

A week later the statement came back in the mail. Across the bottom of the statement the customer had written, HAPPY BIRTHDAY!

Never Serve a Rabbit Stew Before You're Sure You Have the Rabbit

The driver of the automobile was an ardent animal lover and deeply distressed because he ran over a rabbit as he traveled down the highway. As he looked back, he saw the rabbit lying in the road taking its last gasps.

He stopped the car to put the animal out of its misery when another motorist stopped to help. He said he was a salesman for large wholesale drug company and fetched a bottle of tonic from his sample case in his car. He removed the cap from the bottle of tonic and placed it under the nostrils of the hare.

In a few seconds the hare revived and bolted off the highway, across a field and out of sight.

"That's a wonderful tonic," said the animal lover. "What in the world is in that bottle?"

The salesman replied, "Hair restorer!"

Life is a Battle of Wits, and Many People Have to Fight it Unarmed

Hodges and Hillman had been close friends since pharmacy school. They had similar, playful personalities, and were looking for an opportunity to own a pharmacy together.

Hodges found a new shopping complex that was being built next to a large medical complex, and space for a pharmacy was available. He contacted Hillman, and together they leased the space and accomplished their dream: a partnership in a drugstore.

Both of the pharmacists were innovative hard workers and had pleasing personalities. With the aid of the nearby medical complex, they soon developed a thriving business.

Another merchant in the new center had opened his business about the same time, but was not doing well. He asked Hillman to tell him why their pharmacy was such a success.

"Without a doubt," said Hillman, "our success is due to the fact that both Hodges and I take one of our private label vitamin tablets every morning. These vitamins give us the energy and brain power to develop and run this successful pharmacy.

"We personally developed the formula for these vitamins, so we do not have to pay a large royalty to a developer for the product. That is the reason we are able to sell these vitamins for the very low price of $30 for a month's supply."

The merchant was highly impressed and said, "Could I buy a large bottle of these vitamin tablets?" Hillman assured him that he could, and completed the transaction.

About a month later, the merchant returned and

complained to Hillman; "I have been taking these vitamins for a month now and my business hasn't gotten any better!"

"Yes," said Hillman, "but I can see that you are getting smarter!"

The Gift Show

A retail druggist was attending his first gift show to purchase items for the gift department of his newly-opened corner drug store.

One of the more aggressive vendors saw an opportunity to establish a new account, and showered the druggist with attention.

The vendor salesman said, "Why don't we slip down to the bar and I'll buy you a drink?"

"No, thanks," said the druggist, "I don't drink. I tried alcohol once, but I didn't like it."

"Fine," said the vendor, "we can just sit here and visit. Would you like a cigar?"

"Sorry," said the druggist, "I don't smoke. I tried a cigar once, but I didn't care for it."

"That's OK," said the salesman. "After the show rooms close tonight, a group of us are going to play a little poker. Would you care to join us?"

"I'm afraid not," said the druggist, "I'm not a gambler. I tried it once, but it didn't appeal to me. But, my son is with me, maybe he'd like to join in."

The salesman countered, "He's your ONLY son, I assume!"

Just Let George Do It

My friend, pharmacist George Bartholomew, was an enthusiastic outdoorsman and a conservationist. When it came to hunting and fishing, George was among the very best.

The Fish and Game Department frequently consulted him when developing their programs and regulations.

George liked to start the hunting season alone, stake out the location of the game, then invite his friends to accompany him on a hunt. Most of their hunts turned out to be highly memorable and most successful. Many ardent hunters hoped to be invited along.

It was shortly before the opening of the season when George took off alone, back deep into the hills on a three-day stalking trip to locate game. He enjoyed camping in the open and being by himself.

On the second day out, an early snow fall started and gained in intensity. George could see that an early blizzard was imminent and, although he was deep in the back country, he knew the area well. He knew of an abandoned miner's shack in the area and decided to head for it to wait out the storm in comfort.

Back home, however, his wife, Bessie, was quite concerned. The storm had subsided, but the deep snow drifts made normal movement impossible. Bessie contacted the Red Cross. She knew the general area George had headed for, so the Red Cross Rescue Unit took off on a search and rescue mission.

Comfortable in the abandoned shack, George heard the distant bellow horn of the rescue unit faintly announce, "GEORGE, THIS IS THE RED CROSS!" As they drew nearer the shack, the announcement grew in intensity. Finally they neared the shack, but a mammoth snow drift kept the rescue unit at a distance. Again they raised their bellow horn and announced, "GEORGE! THIS IS THE RED CROSS!"

George forced open the front door of the shack, cupped his hands and shouted back, "HECK, MAN, I ALREADY GAVE AT THE DRUG STORE!"

My Mind is Made Up. Don't Confuse Me With the Facts

Three professionals, a surgeon, an architect and a lawyer, were arguing as to whose profession was the oldest.

The surgeon contended that his profession was the oldest because Eve was made from Adam's rib.

"But," countered the architect, "prior to that, order was created out of chaos, and that was an architectual accomplishment."

"And just who," inquired the lawyer, "do you think created the chaos?"

Our Five Senses are Incomplete
Without the Sixth — A Sense of Humor

In an arrangement with the university, we employed pharmacy students during the summer vacation period to give them an opportunity to gain practical experience.

We're in the heart of the ranch country. This is cowboy territory where the men are men and the women are proud of it.

Many of the students were young ladies from the East who had not encountered our kind of customers.

We encouraged the students to be friendly and to offer helpful good service.

One day a dusty old cowboy came into the store. He was bowlegged, sunburned, weather beaten and showed the effects of many years of riding the range.

Our young future pharmacist approached him, and as she gave him a big smile said, "May I help you, sir?" He said, "Yeah, yeah, I wanna get some of that talcum powder!" She gave him another big smile and asked, "Would you walk this way, please?"

He looked at her as she walked away and said, "Young lady, if I could walk that way I wouldn't need that talcum powder!"

Old Salesmen Never Die; The Just Get Out of Commission

Old Tucker was a drug salesman supreme. He had been in the territory for many years, knew his customers well and always led his company's sales force.

Finnigan, the company sales manager, never cared much for Tucker. Finnigan had a reputation for being a hard driver and as cheap as they come. He thought that Tucker's territory should, in reality, produce a much higher sales volume, and that Tucker was lazy and was dragging his feet.

One night while Tucker was out on his territory, he had a heart attack in his motel room and died. The motel manager reluctantly called the drug company and related the tragedy to the sales manager.

Finnigan received the news in a nonchalant manner and told the motel manager, "Return his samples by freight and search his pants for orders."

Some People With Bad Coughs Go to the Doctor; Most Go to the Movie

The patient was admitted to the hospital late in the evening with a very bad cough. When the doctor made his rounds the next morning, he told the patient, "You are coughing much easier this morning."

"I should be," said the patient, "I've been practicing all night."

Few People Travel the Road to Success Without a Puncture or Two

It was 2:30 p.m. on a Wednesday, and an elderly lady entered The Family Pharmacy with a prescription bottle in her hand.

Wilson, the pharmacist, had been in business almost 15 years and this would be the one millionth prescription he had dispensed over the years.

As the lady entered the pharmacy, Wilson saw the prescription bottle in her hand and gave the signal. In response, the lights started flashing on and off, a band began to play, and Wilson stepped forward and pinned an orchid on her dress. With a big smile on his face he pressed a new, crisp $100 bill into her hand. The television cameras were rolling and reporters began interviewing her.

The startled woman was overcome with amazement and asked, "Just what is going on here?"

Wilson was overjoyed and explained to her that the prescription she was about to have refilled would be the one millionth prescription he had dispensed in his near 15 years of business at The  Family Pharmacy. She, as the presenter of that prescription, was being recognized and rewarded.

"Well, really," she stammered, "I'm not having this prescription refilled. I got it filled here last week and it made my husband sick and I'd like to get my money back!"

Most Accidents Happen Accidentally

Wiggins, the pharmacist and his pharmacist wife both worked long hours together in the drug store. They didn't have much of a social life, and what little free time they had was spent at home.

Both of them liked to watch TV but the family room was always cold. They decided to install one of those gas fireplaces with the remote control. A typical pharmacist, Wiggins wanted to save a buck so he installed the fireplace himself.

They were enjoying the comfort of their new fireplace when suddenly there was a gas explosion. The two pharmacists were blown out through a window and landed in the flower bed.

As they got up and dusted themselves off, Wiggin's wife turned to him and said, "You know something? This is the first time we've gone out together for years!"

Cliff Thomas

Memorable Moment in Pharmacy

It was the late 1940s, and I was a new pharmacy graduate following World War II, thanks to the GI Bill. My first job was in a very busy small town pharmacy.

The pharmacist in charge was a lady who had been on the job more than 20 years. She was a seasoned pharmacist, efficient, knowledgeable, and a pleasure to work with.

On the edge of town was a truck garden that was run by two bachelor brothers who were famous for their produce. It had been an ideal season; they had a bumper crop, and it was harvest time.

While having coffee at the soda fountain, I related to one of the brothers a method for freezing sweet corn that I had learned in the service.

By blanching an ear of sweet corn in boiling salt water for three minutes, placing the ear in a condom, adding a teaspoonful of the salt water, tying a knot in the top of the condom and placing it in the freezer, the corn would retain its freshness and flavor all winter long.

I was off duty that weekend, and the brothers decided to give my system a try. Reluctantly and with no explanation, one of the brothers approached the lady pharmacist on Saturday morning to purchase a gross of condoms. Our supply was short but by using several packages of threes, she was able to fill the order.

On Monday morning, the lady pharmacist and I were on duty and our first customer was the brother who had made the Saturday morning purchase. He was extremely unhappy and complained to the lady pharmacist that she had shorted his order by three condoms.

She looked at him in bewilderment and said, "I hope I didn't ruin your weekend!"

Locking Up The Store

It was 10 p.m., and the tired and worn out pharmacist was locking up his drug store after a busy day. As he turned the key in the lock, a boozed up old bum put the touch on him.

"My good man, would you be so kind as to give me $100.50 so I can get a cup of coffee?"

The tired old pharmacist looked at the shabby old recluse and said, "Are you out of your mind? You can get a cup of coffee for 50 cents. What are you going to do with the other $100?"

The bum replied, "Coffee arouses me!"

The Most Dangerous Part of a Car Is the Nut That Holds the Wheel

The young pharmacy student informed his pharmacist father, " Dad, the Bible says that if you don't buy me a car, you don't love me."

"What do you mean? Where in the Bible does it say that?," demanded his father.

"It's right there in Proverbs 13:24, Dad," replied the son. "It says, 'He that spareth the rod hateth his son!'"

Letting the Cat Out of the Bag is Much Easier Than Putting it Back

The customer complained to the pharmacist that she was having a hard time sleeping at night. She said, "The least little sound startles me; I'm sure I'm a victim of insomnia. Even the cat on our back fence disturbs me beyond words. What can I do?"

The pharmacist excused himself and said he would be back in a minute. A short time later he emerged from his sanctum sanctorum with an envelope full of a strange powder.

Handing it to the lady, he said, "This powder will do the trick."

"How do I take it?" asked the customer.

"You don't," said the pharmacist. "Give it to the cat in milk."

Some Men are Driven to Drink But Most Walk to the Bar

A pharmacy student walked into a bar in a university town; he had a 5-pound frog sitting on top of his head.

The bartender looked at him and said, "Where in heck did you get that?"

The frog answered, "Out on the campus of the university. They're all over the place out there."

The Crusty Senior Citizen

Pharmacist Ron had a good reputation for catering to senior citizens. He always gave them special attention at his prescription counter, and he let them know that their business was appreciated. As a result, he did a large prescription volume and owned a thriving pharmacy.

One of his senior citizen customers, old Penfield, complained of severe pain in his right leg. His physician had prescribed a number of treatments and medications but the pain persisted.

The old gent was becoming impatient and said to Ron, "This doctor isn't doing me any good. Can you recommend another one who can give me some help?"

Ron sat his elderly customer down and he began to explain: "Mr. Penfield, you must remember. With advancing age, certain problems arise that you must learn to live with. Remember, that leg is 85 years old."

Penfield looked at Ron and said, "Yeah, but my left leg is the same age and it doesn't bother me."

Some Bosses Take Great Pains
... and Give Them to Others.

The three pharmaceutical manufacturers sales representatives had been friends for years. They were enthusiastic hunters, and had a favorite hunting lodge
where they hunted each fall. Their hunts were always
enormous successes, due to the efforts of a hunting dog
named Salesman, which they engaged at the lodge each
year.

One of the reps told his sales manager about their
annual hunts at the lodge and their great success through
the efforts of Salesman.

The sales manager was impressed, and asked if he
and his friend could arrange a hunt at the same lodge.
The rep advised his boss that there was no problem at
all but be sure to engage the services of the hunting dog
named Salesman.

The next fall, the three detail men arrived for their
annual hunt and asked for their favorite dog, Salesman.

The owner of the lodge growled in disgust, "You don't
want that mutt, he ain't no good any more. Some damn
fool came down here and took him out to hunt. Instead
of calling him "Salesman," he called him "Sales Manager." Now, all he does is sit on his tail and howl!."

47

It's Not a Popular Story

This is one story that all pharmacists hate. Every pharmacist has heard this story a dozen times, and nothing turns them off more. The best way to become very unpopular with a group of pharmacists is to tell this story.

An elderly, hard-of-hearing lady entered the corner drug store and approached the pharmacist to purchase a half-ounce of sweet oil for her ear problem. The pharmacist poured the sweet oil into a dropper bottle, labeled it, put it in the package and said, "That will be one dollar and 50 cents, please." Not hearing well, the lady laid 50 cents on the prescription counter and walked away. The pharmacist called after her, "I said one dollar and 50 cents!" Not understanding him, the lady smiled at him and said, "Yes, and thank you very much," and walked out the door.

Standing there bewildered, the pharmacist looked at the 50 cents in his hand and said to himself, "Oh well, I still made a quarter."

Pharmacists hate that story!

Coming Up Roses

The patient had complained for months about stomach pains. The doctor had examined him thoroughly several times, had run all the tests and even repeated them.

When the doctor couldn't find a problem, he called in an internist for a consultation. After a thorough examination and a battery of tests, still no cause was found, so they decided to operate.

Inside the poor fellow they found a beautiful bouquet of American roses.

"I wonder how those got in there?" said the surgeon.

"I don't know," said the internist. "Look at the card and see who they're from!"

The Classics: Play it Again, Sam

It's a mortal sin of story telling to interrupt the story teller by saying you've already heard that story. You may not realize how long it has taken that person, especially a young child, to gather up enough courage to tell his first story. Don't rain on his parade by not allowing him to test the attempt he has secretly practiced for so long and hard.

Listen to his story and enjoy it . . . again, if necessary. You may learn a new twist on an old favorite, or maybe

— just maybe — you really haven't heard this one before!

A traveling salesman was on his territory. As he approached a small town, he noticed an isolated pharmacy on the edge of the village. The pharmacy was an institution to the local area, and in its second generation was operated by two elderly old maid pharmacists who had inherited it from their pharmacist father.

The salesman had a problem and decided to consult the pharmacist. As he entered the store, he was waited on by one of the sisters. He told her he would like to speak to a registered pharmacist. She explained that both she and her sister were registered pharmacists and that they owned the drug store.

Deciding that perhaps she could help, he explained to her that he had had this strong arousal problem for almost a month, and he had been unable to get rid of it. "What could you give me for it?" he asked.

She said, "That's a rather unusual problem, I'll have to consult with my sister."

She went into the back room and returned in a few minutes. "How about $500 and half the drug store?"

A Laugh a Day Keeps the Psychiatrist Away

Weinand was a relief pharmacist and Patterson owned a small neighborhood pharmacy. Patterson was taking a vacation and Weinand had agreed to fill in for him.

Patterson was a very religious person with a reputation for using strong Christian principles in the operation of his business. Weinand, on the other hand, was a little bit loose and liked to make a buck when he could. As Patterson was leaving to enjoy his vacation he impressed upon the relief pharmacist that he always operated this pharmacy on strictly Christian principles.

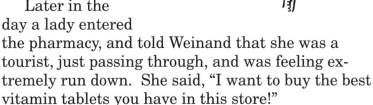

Later in the day a lady entered the pharmacy, and told Weinand that she was a tourist, just passing through, and was feeling extremely run down. She said, "I want to buy the best vitamin tablets you have in this store!"

Weinand selected a small bottle of vitamins made by a reputable manufacturer and said, "This should be a fine vitamin product for you, Madam, and the price is $2.98."

The woman looked at Weinand in disgust and said, "I'll have you know, I am not a pauper, I want something better than that."

Weinand selected another brand and said, "Madam, this is a therapeutic formula of vitamins with all the essential minerals. It's $5.98 a bottle."

Again she looked at Weinand and said, "My good man, my husband is a lawyer, I can afford the very best. I want a bottle of the best vitamins in this store!"

Weinand said, "Just a minute, Madam." In the back room was a new shipment of private label vitamins that Patterson had ordered for over-the-counter sale. The invoice had not arrived so Weinand had no idea of the selling price. He took a bottle and presented it to the lady sayin, "Madam, this is the best bottle of vitamins in the house. It's a private label brand made up special for this pharmacy. It's a therapeutic formula of all the vitamins and it contains a high dose of all the essential minerals. It sells for $30 a bottle," said Weinand.

"That's much better," said the customer. "I'll take it."

When Patterson returned, Weinand related the incident to him and Patterson responded; "How can you rectify Christian principles with that transaction?"

Weinand grinned and said, "She was a stranger and I took her in!"

Roxie Always Has a Funny Story

One of my very favorite pharmacists is my friend, Roxie.

She has a charming twinkle in her eye, and always has a story to tell. Roxie has been putting pills in bottles for more than 10 years and . . . Roxie can call a spade a shovel! I always look forward to seeing her and hearing what she has to say.

Last week, it was my good fortune to be in the area of her pharmacy, so I stopped to see her. Roxie's pharmacy is just across the street from a busy medical center, so it's a very busy pharmacy. People are coming and going all the time, and everybody knows Roxie. She's one of the most popular pharmacists I know.

She said, "You'll never believe what happened across the street last week. Dr. Bingingham, the busiest internist in the clinic, was examining a patient when his nurse rushed in and said, 'Doctor, the man you just gave a clean bill of health walked out of the office and dropped dead. What should I do?'"

The doctor said, "Turn him around so it looks like he just walked in."

The Best Time to Make Friends Is Before You Need Them

A retired 70-year-old pharmacist was walking down the street when she suddenly heard a voice from above boom: "You're going to live to be 100 . . . you're going to live to be 100!"

"Good grief," she said, "if I'm going to make it to 100, I better get this old body repaired." She went to a plastic surgeon and ordered the works. She had it all, a face lift, tummy tucks, lipo suction, the whole nine yards. When she recovered from the operation and left the hospital, she went to the beauty shop and had her hair dyed and restyled.

As she was leaving the beauty shop and crossing the street, she was run over by a large cattle truck and died.

When she arrived at the Golden Gate, she was indeed unhappy. St. Peter tried to welcome her but she was angry.

"I thought you said I would live to be 100?," she screamed.

St. Peter replied, "I didn't recognize you!"

Some Days You Are The Pigeon, Some Days You Are The Statue

Two well-dressed pharmaceutical sales representatives were walking down the street of a large city. They were on their way to a plush hotel to attend the regional sales meeting of their pharmaceutical company.

Their company was a world leader in the manufacture of pharmaceutical products, and the annual event recognized the company's outstanding sales persons for that year.

The two sales representatives were discussing possible winners of the award. As luck would have it, a pigeon flying overhead made a dropping at the precise moment necessary to strike the head of one of the detail men.

The receiver of the deposit said to his companion, "That pigeon just went on my head. Do you have a handkerchief so I can wipe it?".

The other salesman replied, "Don't be ridiculous! That pigeon must be a mile away by now!"

Planting Time

Don, one of my very good pharmacist friends, is retired from the United States Public Health Service. His final assignment was at a federal penitentiary, where he served as a pharmacist for 17 years. He has many great stories to relate about this assignment, and here is one of his favorites:

A convict was serving a 10-year sentence for robbing a bank. It was well-known that all of the inmates' incoming and outgoing mail was censored, so he had to be very careful of the things he wrote about.

One day he received a letter from his wife wanting to know how she could dig up the garden to plant the potatoes.

He wrote back, saying, "Don't dig up the garden; that's where I hid the money!"

A couple of weeks later his wife wrote back, "The sheriff and four of his deputies were out here yesterday and dug up every bit of the garden."

The inmate wrote back, "Now, plant the potatoes!"

Professional Service Representatives

Three pharmacy professional service representatives got stranded together in a small town during a blizzard. All three were staying in the same motel, so they met in the bar that evening.

The first detail man was an Irishman, originally from Boston, who said, "Back in Boston, we have an Irish pub called O'Leary's. When you buy the first drink and the second drink, O'Leary gives you the third drink on the house."

The second rep was an Italian from New York. He said, "Back in Brooklyn, we have an Italian bar called Julio's. You pay for the first drink and the second drink, and after you have paid for the third drink, for the rest of the night all your drinks are free."

The third rep was Polish and from Chicago. He said, "Back in Chicago, where I come from, we have a bar called Slavinskie's. At this bar you get your first drink free, your second drink free, and your third drink free. Then, four guys take you back to their apartment and they entertain you the whole weekend."

The Irish rep and the Italian rep were amazed. They couldn't believe what they were hearing. The Irishman said, "Man, that's almost unbelievable. Did that really happen to you?"

"Well, not to me personally," said the Polish rep, "But it did happen to my sister."

Retirement is Wonderful if You
Have Two Essentials:
Much to Live On, and Much to Live For

Todd, the pharmacist, had retired from active practice. He had operated his community pharmacy for 40 years, working six to seven days a week and 10 to 12 hours a day.

He soon found out that he woke up in the morning with nothing to do, and by bedtime he only had it half done. His new life style was more than he could cope with. His constant companionship was driving his wife mad.

Attempting to give herself some relief, she suggested that Todd take up fishing.

He followed through on her suggestion but this only created more problems. Finally, in desperation, she called a friend who was a psychiatrist. "You've got to come over right away," pleaded the wife. "My husband's in terrible shape. Please hurry."

The psychiatrist arrived and asked where the husband was. "He's down the hall in the last room on the left. He's been there all week." The doctor rushed down the hall, looked in the room and saw the pharmacist sitting in the bathroom sink with a fishing line dangling in the bathtub.

"You're absolutely right," said the doctor, "Why on earth didn't you call me sooner?"

"I would have," said the wife, "but I've been cleaning fish all week!"

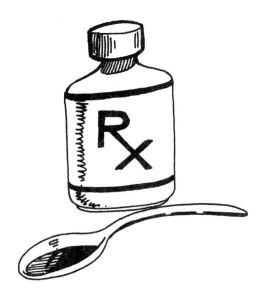

School is the Mouse Race
That Equips You for the Rat Race

Sister Madelon was conducting the first day of class for her new third-grade students. To get everyone acquainted, she announced that she would call on students to introduce themselves. Students were to stand, give their names, and tell what their daddies did. Then, they were to spell his line of work, business, or profession, and tell the class what their daddies would do for them if they were to visit the class today.

Little Mary was called on first, and she stood and said, "My name is Mary Smith and my daddy is a doctor, d-o-c-t-o-r. If he visited us today, he would make anyone who is sick well again."

"That was very good, Mary," said Sister Madelon. Next she called on Betty Jones.

"Betty stood and said, "My name is Betty Jones and my daddy is a pharmacist, f-a-r —, p-a-r —." It was obvious that Betty was having a problem with the spelling.

Sister Madelon said, "Betty, why don't you sit down and think about that spelling for a while, and I will call on you again. I am sure you can get it right."

Next she called on Bennie Bastoni, and Bennie said, "My name is Bennie Bastoni and my dad is a bookie, that's b-o-o-k-i-e. If he visited us today, he would lay you eight to five that Betty ain't ever going to be able to spell pharmacist."

The Higher You Get at Night, the Lower You Feel in the Morning

The visiting pharmacist walked into the small country bar and was highly impressed with the rustic decor, especially the sawdust on the floor.

He ordered a drink and said to the bartender, "Why do you put sawdust on the floor?" The bartender said, "That's not sawdust. It's yesterday's furniture."

The Only Thing Stronger Than a Mother's Love Sometimes is a Father's Breath

The pharmacist was out of town attending a convention when his wife came down with a cold. Unable to talk to her husband about a treatment, she remembered an old-fashioned remedy that her mother used to use. It was a glass of hot whiskey in water with honey and lemon juice.

A short time later her little daughter was ready for bed, so her mother took her to her bedroom to tuck her in and give her a goodnight kiss.

The daughter looked at her mother and said, "Mother! You've been using daddy's perfume!"

The Horse You Put Your Money On Usually Runs Away With It

Pharmacist Winston didn't mind a little wager now and then. In fact, he would bet the sun wouldn't come up tomorrow morning if you gave him good odds. He had never been to a race track, never had bet on the horses, until he took a vacation to Kentucky.

Four was always his lucky number. He was born on April 4, he had four children, and he lived at 444 4th Street in the fourth largest city in the state he lived. He went to the races on his 44th birthday, and was surprised to find a horse named "July 4th," running in the fourth race. He went to window 4 and put $4,000 on the horse named July 4th.

Sure enough, the horse came in fourth!

The Pet Shop

The superstore had a small in-store pet shop where they sold a variety of birds and fish.

An epidemic broke out among the birds, and many canaries began to die.

A veterinarian was called in to determine the nature of the problem. She made a study and gave her diagnosis:

"It's chirpes, that's a canerial disease, and it's untweetable."

The Doctor is in Charge

I do some pharmacy relief work in an area hospital when they need extra help to cover for sick leaves, vacations, or when they get extra busy. It's a busy community hospital in a small town, so the staff is a close-knit group.

The other day, I was walking down the hall with the director of nurses, who was showing me the proposed location for the new and enlarged pharmacy.

As we passed the emergency room, we could hear a doctor shouting, "INSULIN STAT! TETANUS! GAMMA GLOBULIN AT ONCE!"

I looked at the nursing director in amazement and asked, "What is that all about?"

She smiled and said, "The doctor is the captain of the team. That's another physician calling the shots!"

Pharmacy in the Public Health Service

My friend, Pharmacist Ted, spent many years in the United States Public Health Service. For a number of those years, he was assigned to the Indian Health Service. He is now retired and enjoys telling about his many professional experiences.

For a time, Ted was the chief pharmacist in an IHS hospital on a large reservation. Many young physicians, just out of medical school, were assigned to reservation hospitals where Ted was stationed. They were required to serve two years at a "hardship" post to repay the federal government for financial assistance the government had supplied for their medical education. These were busy hospitals, and these young physicians worked their tails off keeping up with the rapid pace.

One afternoon, while all the pharmacists were busy preparing prescriptions, a young physician ducked into the pharmacy to hide for a bit to catch some rest. He needed a break from the hustle and bustle of the busy hospital clinic.

As the young physician watched Ted perform his duties, he said, "I wish I were a pharmacist. You pharmacists really have a nifty job. You do neat things."

Ted responded by asking, "Did you take a 4-year premed course before you went to medical school?"

The doctor responded that he had.

"That makes you very fortunate indeed," said Ted. "If you take three more years of pharmacy classes, you could move up to being a pharmacist."

Behind Every Successful Man Stands an Amazed Mother-in-Law

Pharmacist O'Toole never was a big winner with his mother-in-law. From the start, she didn't feel that he was good enough for her daughter.

O'Toole hung in there, however, and was always working on things he might do to please her.

It was his birthday, and out of courtesy to her daughter, the mother-in-law sent O'Toole a gift of two neckties, one red and the other blue.

The following week, the mother-in-law came to visit. When the mother-in-law arrived, O'Toole's wife immediately brought her to the drug store to see O'Toole, behind his prescription counter, wearing the red necktie.

She looked at him and barked, "What's the matter? Didn't you like the blue one?"

If at First You Don't Succeed, Try Doing it the Way Your Wife Told You

Being a conservative pharmacist, Dale decided he would save a few bucks by painting his own house. During the process, he fell off the ladder and cracked his head on the concrete driveway below. A swelling developed and he had a terrific headache. Since his wife wasn't home, he drove himself to the emergency room.

After the examination, the doctor advised him that hot compresses would reduce the swelling and relieve the pain.

When his wife returned home, she found her husband with a hot-water bottle strapped on his head. He explained to her what had happened and the advice the doctor had given him.

His wife looked at him with disgust and said, "Cold packs are best for a swelling and a headache." She gave him an ice pack.

In no time at all, Dale's headache was gone and the swelling was reduced.

The pharmacist was quite unhappy and phoned the doctor. "You told me to use *hot packs* on my head, and my wife told me to use *cold packs*. Her treatment was better!"

The doctor said, "My wife says *hot packs!*"

The Office Nurse

Rosemary is the office nurse for a local physician. They have been working together for a number of years. She calls our pharmacy several times a day to relay prescriptions or to request information. Over the years, Rosemary and I have become good friends, so I always look forward to hearing from her.

The physician has a reputation for being able to call a spade a shovel, and Rosemary tries her best to keep things in the office running as smoothly as possible.

One day, the doctor instructed Rosemary to get an old colleague of his on the phone. As she lifted the phone to dial that number, she discovered an incoming call already on the line. It was one of their elderly woman patients wishing to speak to the doctor.

It was obvious to Rosemary that this was an urgent call, so she put the woman right through to the doctor. Thinking it was his old friend on the line, the doctor picked up the phone and boomed out, "Hello, you old X@##X!&?! How the hell are you?"

What to Eat in Hot Weather is a Problem to Some People, but What to Eat in All Kinds of Weather is a Problem to Others

If you haven't been a member of our profession long enough to have experienced the soda fountain, you missed some glorious times in pharmacy. If you have, you know what I mean.

In the days of the drugstore luncheonette, a registered pharmacist really had to know his onions. Operating a luncheonette was an exacting science.

You were never looked upon as a first class druggist if you put too much salt in your tunafish salad sandwiches.

A million stories have evolved from the soda fountain. After all these years, a few are still easy to recall:

A fellow seated himself at the soda fountain and inquired of the waitress, "What flavors of ice cream to you have?"

The girl's throat was inflamed, so she answered in a raspy voice, "Vanilla, chocolate and maple nut."

He looked at her in bewilderment and inquired. "Do you have laryngitis?"

"No, just vanilla, chocolate and maple nut."

How do I take these pills?

Being the compliance officer for our board of pharmacy takes me into many different pharmacy settings. When Yogi said, "You can observe a lot by watching," he was absolutely correct. This is one story that I honestly can vouch for, because I watched it develop.

I was in a very busy pharmacy doing a controlled substance audit for the Drug Enforcement Authority. They require such an audit as a condition of the license. These audits are intense and take a lot of time. A little tension-breaker can be a great reward.

A young lady approached the pharmacy counter and presented an empty birth control tablet packet requesting a refill. When the pharmacist entered the prescription number into the computer, it came up as third-party-pay prescription. The computer rejected the prescription as an early refill.

The pharmacist explained to the patient that her insurance program required that the prescription be filled in quantities of a three-month supply. Since the prescription was filled six weeks ago, she should still have a six-week supply on hand from the original prescription. The patient looked very bewildered and asked, "How would they know that?"

The pharmacist went on to explained that the original prescription contained 84 tablets, and that she was to take one tablet each day. Therefore, the prescription would last 84 days, roughly three months.

The patient, with eyes wide, asked, "You mean I don't take one each time?"

The Second Thing to Go is Your Memory

A retired pharmacist was having trouble with his memory. He couldn't remember anything, and his wife was having trouble with her memory, too.

He was reading the paper one evening, and he read an ad about the memory doctor, who could help restore one's memory. He called his wife over and told her to read the ad. She thought it sounded pretty good and said, "I think we ought to see that doctor."

He said, "I think we should, too." So, they went to see the memory doctor.

They had been going to the doctor for about six weeks when they went down to the senior citizen center and ran into one of their old friends. The friend said, "I understand you're going to the memory doctor."

The pharmacist said, "Yes, that's right, we're both going."

"Is he any good?"

"Is he any good?!," said the pharmacist. "He's the best doctor we've ever been to; he's really good."

His friend said, "You know, I'm having trouble with my memory, too. I think I ought to see that doctor. What's his name?"

The pharmacist hesitated, "What's the doctor's name? . . . What's the doctor's name? Look, there's a flower with a real long stem and the stem has little green leaves and there are thorns sticking out on the stem. Then, at the top of the stem is a big bulb flower that comes in all different colors. What do you call that?"

His friend said, "Why, that's a rose."

The pharmacist said, "Yeah, that's right, rose." He turned to his wife and said, "Hey, Rose, what's the name of that doctor we've been going to?"

Two is Company, Three is the Result

It was a quiet afternoon in the pharmacy, so I had some time to catch up on a few things for a change. I was placing some orders by telephone when a young lady approached the prescription counter. She presented a prescription from an obstetrician for prenatal tables, so I knew she was in the early stages of pregnancy.

I was making pleasant conversation when she said, "Could I use your telephone, please? I would like to call my husband at his office."

I wanted to share the good news and I willingly granted permission by inviting her into the prescription department to make the call. Since I was standing next to her, I could not help but overhear the conversation.

She got her husband on the line and said, "You dirty rat, you got me pregnant."

The husband answered in amazement, "To whom am I speaking, please?"

BANKER

The Glass-Eyed Banker

Ask any community pharmacist and they will tell you, it's vital for success to have a friendly working relationship with the banker. If you want to keep that corner drug store afloat, you better pamper old money bags.

My friend, pharmacist Casey, runs a good show, and learned this lesson well. He was getting ready for Christmas, his harvest season, and was about to go to market to do the buying. This triggered his annual visit to the banker. It's a cold-hearted encounter and takes some planning to meet face to face with the ruthless one.

Casey had done his homework and carefully laid out his plan; how much he would need, what he would buy, and how he would pay it back.

After some discussion the banker said, "It sounds like a reasonable workable plan, I'll tell you what I'll do. One of my eyes is a glass eye. If you can tell me which eye is glass, I'll make you the loan."

Casey didn't bat an eye. "It's your left eye," he replied.

"You're right," said the banker, "but how did you know?"

Again Casey was prompt with his answer. "I thought I detected a drop of human kindness in that left eye."

The Most Difficult Years of a Marriage Are Those Following the Wedding

Pharmacist Finnigan and his wife were celebrating their golden wedding anniversary. Their church held a celebration for them, and it was obvious that they were happily married and enjoyed each other's company.

A newly-married couple who were at the celebration were very impressed with the success of this long marriage, and asked the elderly couple for the secret of their marital longevity.

The old pharmacist was delighted with all the attention of the celebration and was more than willing to share their secret.

With a twinkle in his eye, the knowledgeable old druggist replied, "Well, Sonny, I'll tell you. I've always treated Ma in such a fashion that if I should have died, it would have taken more than a hot water bottle to replace me."

The Kindly Old Pharmacist

Mr. Jones was a kind, fatherly-looking old pharmacist from the old school. He became a pharmacist in the early 1930s when a six month course was the requirement for registration.

Mr. Jones had been employed in the same neighborhood drug store for more than 30 years. While the ownership changed a number of times, Mr. Jones was always there, taking care of the people. He was an institution in the neighborhood, and he had served some of the families into the second and third generation.

A stickler for good health practices, Mr. Jones insisted that his customers take their vitamins every day. When someone would come in to purchase a product for a rundown condition, Mr. Jones would stress that a daily vitamin tablet would have prevented this problem.

Henry, a pharmaceutical service representative for one of the major drug companies, had convinced Mr. Jones some time earlier that his company's therapeutic multiple vitamins were the very best vitamin product on the market. As a result, Mr. Jones always recommended the vitamin product marketed by Henry's company.

On every occasion, Mr. Jones would talk up that vitamin product to his patrons. It soon became the most popular vitamin product in the entire area. People would stop in at the drug store to buy their vitamins from Mr. Jones, sometimes even one tablet at a time. The store ordered the vitamin tablets in bottles of 100 in lots of three to five gross at a time. The sales just kept on growing.

As a direct result of Mr. Jones' efforts, Henry, the drug salesman, won all the sales contests and was named his company's top vitamin salesman in the nation three years in a row.

To show his appreciation, Henry brought his regional manager to the drug store to meet Mr. Jones and to personally thank him for his efforts on behalf of their vitamin product. To further show his appreciation, the regional manager presented Mr. Jones with a bottle of 1,000 tablets of the popular vitamin tablets for his very own use.

Deeply appreciative, Mr. Jones thanked them profusely for the vitamins, looked them both in the eye and invited them into the back room.

After closing the door and being sure that only the three of them were in on the conversation, Mr. Jones turned to the regional manager and said, "You know, I've got a bad heart. There isn't anything in these tablets that will hurt me, is there?"

The Exhausted Pharmacist

Nobody, but nobody, puts in a day like the retail pharmacist. After as much as 12 hours behind his prescription counter, serving his customers, filling prescriptions, saving lives, he's exhausted and ready to relax.

My friend and pharmacist, Timothy, was no different. He had just finished a full day behind his prescription counter. It was a hot summer day, and he was ready for a cold beer, so he stopped at his favorite bar.

As he was sitting there, trying to relax a bit, a woman came in and sat down at the bar a few stools away. Timothy looked her way. She gave him a big smile and then motioned for him to come over and sit next to her. He moved over to the stool next to her, and she gave him a big come-on smile as they exchanged pleasant conversation.

After some light talk, she turned to him and said, "I'm a working girl, if you know what I mean. Business has been slow, so I'll offer you a very special deal. For $50, I'll do anything you want."

"Anything?," exclaimed the pharmacist.

She leaned close to him, looked into his eyes and whispered, "Yes, for $50 I'll do anything you like."

"OK," said Timothy, "paint my house!"

The Minor Surgical Procedure

A straitlaced circulating nurse in the community hospital where I do pharmacy relief work related this story to me, so I assume it's for real.

A very attractive young lady was about to go through a minor surgical procedure. My friend, the float nurse, had wheeled her to the operating room door and left her there, while she went in to see if the surgical staff was ready.

Pretty soon, a young man in a white coat came up to the patient cart, lifted the sheet, examined her closely and walked away, nodding his head in approval. A short time later, another man came to the scene and did a similar examination without comment.

When a third man appeared and pulled back the sheet, she inquired, "Why all the last minute examinations? Has there been a change of plans, is there a problem? Aren't they going to go ahead with the operation?"

"I have no idea, lady," the young man replied. "We're just painting the hallway."

There's a Reason They Put Erasers on Pencils

Craft died and went to heaven. As he approached the golden gate he announced to St. Peter, "I have arrived."

St. Peter said, "I'll have to check the master book, it's just a formality, what is your name?"

"Kenneth Craft," announced the new arrival.

St. Peter checked the book twice, shook his head and said, "You're not in the book, I'm afraid you're in the wrong place."

"That's not possible," the surprised Craft said, " there has to be a mistake. Would you please check the book again, I'm sure I belong here."

St. Peter checked the book again and sure enough, near the back of the book he found Craft's name. "You belong here alright," St. Peter said, "but you weren't expected to arrive for 20 more years. Tell me, who is your pharmacist?"

The Pharmacist with a Problem

The doctor had been treating Murphy for a couple of weeks but Murphy still suffered with constipation.

"Your condition really has me stumped," said the doctor.

"Tell me, what do you do for a living?"

"I'm a pharmacist," said Murphy.

The doctor took out his billfold, handed Murphy a $10 bill and said, "That figures. Here, go and get something to eat!"

The Dying Pharmacist

Pharmacist Stanley had done his three score and ten and realized he was about to cross over the great divide.

The doctor had told his wife that Stanley was dying, so she went into the bedroom to see him.

"I'm going to see the Lord," said the pharmacist. "But before I go, could I have a piece of your delicious chocolate cake I can smell in the oven?"

"Certainly not," said the wife, "we're saving it for the funeral."

The Luncheonette

We had a very busy lunch counter in our corner drug store. The fountain manager was a crafty old gal, who could hold her own with the best of them. In addition to being a great cook, she could also bake a mean pie. She was famous for her pies which she could bake in any flavor. Her great talent drew customers to our drug store from throughout the area. Over the years she also developed a very special sandwich. She was very proud of this sandwich and called it "the super special."

It was a delightful treat with a highly successful reputation and she always featured this sandwich on Wednesdays. In fact, each Wednesday, it was a contest to exceed the sales of "the super special" the previous Wednesday. This was usually accomplished and the sales volume just kept climbing.

One Wednesday noon a stranger came in and took a seat at the counter and said, "I'd like a ham sandwich, please."

She said, "I'm sorry, Sir, on Wednesday we feature the super special. It has ham, cheese, salami, peppers, pickles, onions and lettuce. It's very good."

"Please," he answered, "all I want is a ham sandwich."

"OK, Sir," she frowned, "Mildred! One super special. Hold the cheese, salami, peppers, pickles, onions and lettuce."

76

The Military Pharmacist

Arthur was a young military pharmacist just out of the college ROTC program. He was a quiet man who kept to himself. He was the officer in charge of the pharmacy, did his job efficiently, and didn't fraternize much with the rest of the staff. He wasn't particularly liked or disliked by the other staff members and, in general, the pharmacy operated smoothly.

However, Arthur did have one habit that puzzled the staff, and it was a constant subject of wonder. Upon his arrival each morning he would enter his office, unlock the center drawer of his desk, peek into the drawer, then close the door, and relock it. This was a ritual that happened every morning and never varied. Once he relocked the door, his daily duties began.

Everyone in the pharmacy wondered what the contents of the drawer might be and that was a frequent subject of conversation at coffee breaks, lunch, and social events. Everyone wondered what was in the desk drawer, but no one had a clue as to what it might be.

Finally, one day, Arthur departed on a 10-day vacation and, to everyone's amazement, he left his office door unlocked and the desk drawer wide open for all to see. About midmorning one of the staff members noticed the open drawer, and word soon spread throughout the dispensary. In no time, more than a dozen staff members had gathered outside the office hoping to find some answers.

With quite a bit of coaxing, the sergeant advanced and entered the office to examine the mysterious desk drawer. On first glance, the drawer appeared empty, but further examination revealed a piece of paper pasted to the bottom of the drawer. The paper contained a single sentence. As the audience stood spellbound, the sergeant read the message aloud: "OS means the left eye."

The Military Professor

I enrolled in pharmacy at the university in the fall of 1945. My class of 38 students included four young women and four young men who had just graduated from high school and were not veterans. The remaining 30 were recently discharged from the military and were attending college under the newly-enacted GI Bill.

These were seasoned veterans who had seen a lot of military action in the different branches of the service. They varied in age from 22 to 49. Many were married and had young families. Some had children who were attending the same university.

Our professor of pharmaceutical chemistry was a recently-discharged captain who held a Ph.D. in chemistry and had served three years stateside in the army Chemical Warfare Department. He was very proud of his rank and his stateside duty and frequently wore his military uniform with the captain's bars as he taught his classes. He was a stickler for perfection, and enjoyed dressing down the older students for minor imperfections.

His lectures were peppered with phrases such as: "When I was in the military . . . ," or, "When I was promoted to the rank of captain . . . ," or, "The soldiers that I commanded . . . ," and, "My military experience has taught me . . . ," these seasoned veterans soon tired of his efforts at self-glorification.

One afternoon we were in the chemistry lab and Bob, my lab partner, had a minor accident and created a mess with no serious consequences. The professor made a big issue of this and humiliated poor Bob in front of the class.

"Didn't you learn anything about cleaning up a mess when you were in the service, Mister?"

Bob gave him a stern look and said, "Sir, when I was in the service I had captains who cleaned up after me!"

The next day, Bob showed up for class wearing his military uniform. He was a fighter pilot, and had commanded a fighter group in the Army Air Corps. His rank was full colonel, and his tunic carried a command pilot's wings and two rows of military decorations. Bob had been wounded in action and had shot down several enemy planes.

Our chemistry professor never wore his captain's uniform to class again, and for the next three years his military service was not mentioned.

The Party Invitation

This story was told to me by a wine merchant, who kept things bottled up inside. He finally blew his cork.

A society lady, who was famous for her lavish dinner parties, sent an invitation to the community's leading internist inviting him to her dinner party.

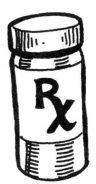

The doctor replied with a poorly hand-written illegible note. She showed it to her husband saying, "I can't read this note, I have no idea if he has accepted or refused."

The husband looked at the note and said, " I'll take it to the pharmacy, a pharmacist can always read a doctor's handwriting."

Approaching the pharmacist, the husband said, "Can you interpret this for me?"

The pharmacist looked at the message and said, "Give me a few minutes, I'll be right back," and disappeared into the back room. He returned in a few minutes with a small bottle.

"Here you are," he said. "That will be $22.50."

The Secret of Repartee is Repartee

Northgate had practiced community pharmacy for 40 years. He was a good businessman and a good pharmacist and was able to retire in a fairly comfortable style. Still, in spite of his success, he never quite reached the financial goal he had set for himself when he entered the profession.

For as long as he could remember he was haunted with the perplexing question: WHAT IS THE SECRET FOR SUCCESS IN PHARMACY?

He searched everywhere for the answer. At meetings and conventions and at any association with other pharmacists, he always proposed the question, but never found the answer.

While operating his pharmacy, he visited with every successful salesman who called on him, seeking an answer, but never able to find it. On the day of his retirement, the question remained unanswered and he was now even more determined to find it. In fact, on that day he set a goal for himself to search for the answer until he found it.

After a year of thinking, searching, and reading, he learned of a lama who lived alone on a mountain top in Tibet. This holy man had spent 40 years in prayer and meditation, and was said to be able to answer any question proposed to him.

After much investigation, Northgate realized that the answer to his question lay in a visit to the mountaintop and a consultation with the lama. He realized that such a journey would be dangerous and expensive, but he was driven to do so.

Northgate sold everything he owned to raise the capital and started on his journey to seek the counsel of the lama. He flew to Tibet, hired a team of professional guides and began his trek to the mountaintop.

The journey to the mountaintop was hard and treacherous. When less than half completed, the guides confessed that the journey was too much for them. If he insisted on continuing the trip, he would have to go on by himself. Obsessed with his goal, Northgate continued on alone, with only enough food to sustain himself. Enduring the elements he was able to climb a few hours a day and finally, after a month of climbing, he reached the mountain top. There, sitting on the raw stone at the peak of the mountain, sat the lama, staring into the distance and saying not a word.

Approaching the holy man, Northgate stood before him, bowed from the waist and said, "Oh Holy One, I have struggled and sacrificed everything I owned to journey to this spot to request an audience with you. You are the only one who can help me."

The holy man turned to Northgate and said, "I know of your journey and the difficulties you have overcome, and your request is granted. What is your question?"

"Oh, Most Holy One," Northgate continued, "all of my life I have sought this answer but no one has been able to supply it. Please tell me, what is the secret to success in pharmacy?"

The lama sat still for several minutes and then turned his head toward Northgate, looked him straight in the eye and said, "My son, the secret to success in pharmacy is a simple one. Buy low and sell high."

With Proper Care, the Human Body Will Last a Lifetime

The doctor was called to the home of Shroll, the pharmacist. He had suddenly taken ill, and was confined to bed.

The doctor went into the bedroom, while Shroll's wife waited outside for the doctor's report.

After nearly half an hour, the doctor came out of the bedroom with a look of deep concern on his face.

"I must be honest with you, Mrs. Shroll," the doctor said. "I don't like the way your husband looks, at all."

"Well," replied the wife, "neither do I, but he's always been nice to the kids."

To Err is Human; to Forget ... Routine

A retired pharmacist and his wife were watching TV late one evening, when the pangs of hunger hit him and he got up to get some ice cream.
His wife said, "Get me some, too. Write it down!"

As he headed for the kitchen, she added, "Put some chocolate syrup on it. Write it down!" After a couple of more steps she called after him, "Put some crushed nuts on it. Write it down!"

Several minutes later he returned to the TV set with a plate of scrambled eggs. She looked up and said, "What's that?"

He said, "I brought your eggs." She said, "You forgot the bacon. I told you to write it down!"

In the Use of Words, Quality is More Important Than Quantity

We had a very active Toastmaster's club in our little city that met every Monday at 7 a.m. Most of the members were businessmen on Main Street, so this early hour meeting allowed us to be back in our stores when the day began.

At one meeting, the Toastmaster called for some extemporaneous talks. He wrote a number of subjects on a piece of paper and called on several members to draw a subject from the hat. They were to speak on that subject for five minutes extemporaneously.

My friend, Willard, the banker, drew a subject and it read, "SEX". In spite of it being a difficult subject, he did quite well with his assignment.

That evening his wife said, "How did Toastmaster's go?"

He said, "I got quite a surprise. I had to give a five minute extemporaneous speech and I wasn't expecting it."

"What did you talk about?" she asked.

He didn't want to go into a lot of detail, so he said, "Sailing a sailboat."

A couple of days later, his wife came into the drug store and I said, "Marie, Willard did a terrific job at Monday morning Toastmasters with a very difficult subject."

She said, "That's what I understand. But really, I don't know how he could know much about it. He only tried it twice. The first time he got seasick and the second time his hat blew off!"

The Visiting Pharmacist

Pharmacist Larson had just purchased a drug store in a small farming community and wanted to meet some of his potential customers.

After talking to some of the other merchants on Main Street, he decided to take a few days off and drive through the countryside and introduce himself. Outside an old weather-beaten farm house, he saw a man milking a cow and stopped to meet him.

The conversation just got under way when the farmer's wife appeared on the front porch of the farm house. "Ike, you get in this house, and who is that guy you're talking to?" the wife said.

"He's the new druggist, Ma," Ike answered.

"In that case," said his wife, "you better bring the cow inside with you."

You Can't Make a Fast Buck on a Slow Horse

Swen, the pharmacist, owned a race horse. He couldn't make a buck in the drug business so he thought he would try the track. He entered his horse and was very unhappy after the race. Swen demanded of the jockey, "You lost the race, what happened?"

"Well," said the jockey, "at least I didn't come in last, there were two horses behind me."

Swen replied in disgust, "They were first and second in the next race!"

84

The Way Some Fishermen Catch Fish is by the Tale

My pharmacist friend, Bill Husband, is one of the funniest people I know. Customers come and go in his pharmacy, and they usually go out happier than they came in. Bill has a sly sense of humor and graciously shares it with his customers. People love him for it and he has built a thriving business just being himself.

Besides being a good pharmacist, he is also an ardent fisherman. When he has time for leisure activity, he loves to invade a trout stream and give it a go.

Near my summer cabin in the Black Hills of South Dakota is a marvelous trout stream that not many people know about. I invited Bill to spend a weekend at the cabin and give the stream a try.

The second day out, Bill encountered an individual along the stream who inquired, "Any luck this morning?"

"No," replied Bill, "it has been pretty quiet, but I laid them dead yesterday. I've never seen anything like it. I caught a dozen before noon, took them to the cabin and had another dozen by three o'clock. I took those to the cabin and went out again and had another dozen before the sun went down. Best day of fishing I ever had."

"Do you know who I am?," asked the stranger.

"I have no idea," said Bill

"I am a warden with the South Dakota Department of Game and Fish," said the stranger.

"Do you have any idea who I am?," asked Bill.

"I have no idea," said the warden.

Bill replied, "I'm the biggest liar in South Dakota."

They Call Me a Dreamer; Maybe I Am

You can call it nostalgia if you want to, but I miss the "good old days." I miss the dime store, the ice man, train trips and the Saturday afternoon matinee. But most of all, I miss the real drug store with the soda fountain, cherry Cokes and racks of comic books.

You can say what you want, but we lost a lot when we abandoned the soda fountain. We pharmacists lost the fellowship of really getting to know our customers. The customers lost the town meeting place, the community social center.

Nostalgia? I guess so! Small town? Perhaps! Old fashioned? Well maybe!

In the hectic confusion of the modern drug store, it would be nice to experience a few dull moments occasionally. Every pharmacist ought to sit back, close his eyes, and meditate for a while each day and try not to snore! When I think back to the soda fountain days, I always come up with a chuckle. That's why I'm so keen on periods of meditation each day. Something always comes back, like this one:

I hired a young pharmacist whose name was Ralph. He had just graduated from pharmacy college. The first day on the job he told me, "I want to learn the drug business from the bottom up!"

I said, "Ralph, I will teach you the drug business from the bottom up, but to do that, you must start behind the soda fountain!" In those days the soda fountain was the heart of the drug store.

At the soda fountain we sold prepackaged ice cream. We had quarts of chocolate, strawberry and vanilla. Ralph got into the very bad habit of cutting these quarts in half. Customers would ask for a half quart of chocolate and a half quart of vanilla and he would cut the quarts in half. It was raising Cain with my profit picture at the soda fountain because I was getting stuck with the other half.

I said, "Ralph, I don't want any more of this! We will no longer sell half of this and half of that. Now, if you don't feel comfortable telling these customers no, you bring them back to me and I will tell them. But, no more!"

A little while after that a big old cowboy came in. He was about 6'-4" and weighed about 285. He said, "I want to get a half quart of chocolate and a half quart of vanilla."

Ralph said, "I'm sorry, we don't do that any more."

The cowboy said, "What do you mean, you don't do that any more? I've been buying it right along. Get with it, Buster"

Ralph came back to me and said, "Look, I've got some big, dumb, stupid cowboy up there and he wants to get a half quart of chocolate and a half quart of vanilla." Ralph glanced over his shoulder and the cowboy was standing right behind him!

Ralph gave him a sheepish grin and said, "And this gentleman would like to buy the other half."

The Woman Who Knows All the Answers Never Gets Asked

The pharmacy tech sent her clothes to the laundry and called to complain. "I received six pair of men's sox in my bundle and I'm not even married!"

The lady at the laundry replied, "We're really sorry, we'll send a man out right away!"

You Can't Tell One Player from Another Without a Score Card

Each year, before the Christmas buying market, the corner drug store had an inventory adjustment sale. This annual event was always the biggest sale of the year, and was looked forward to by all the customers in the shopping area.

On the morning of the big sale a long line had formed in front of the drug store. A small man pushed his way to the front of the line and upset a number of people. With some derogatory remarks and some disparaging shoves, he was pushed to the back of the line.

On his second attempt, several women pushed and shoved him and actually physically carried him to the back of the line and deposited him on the ground with much force. In no uncertain terms he was told to stay there.

As he got up and brushed himself off he announced to the group assembled: "That does it! This is the last time. If you rough-house me one more time, I'm not opening the drug store."

Wall Drug

In the early 1930s, pharmacist Ted Hustead and his wife, Dorothy, staked their claim in the Badlands of western South Dakota. They cashed in on the dusty western plains with free ice water to establish what has become the most famous drug store in the world: Wall Drug.

Ted and I have been friends for years, and in addition to a flair for promotion, he has a marvelous sense of humor.

This is a story Ted told to me some time ago, and I will relate it just as he told it:

This group of small town merchants agreed to work together in an effort to improve business for all of them. Since they were a close-knit group and knew each other well, each merchant who had a store agreed to give credit to the families of the other merchants.

One afternoon, the son of the butcher rushed into his father's shop and announced that his mother had sent him.

"There's a bill collector at our house and mama says for you to come home right away and pay him."

"Which one of the merchants is trying to collect, son?" asked the butcher.

"I don't know which one it is, but mama said that he wants his money right away."

"Well, son, you tell your mother that I will be home shortly. Then, you whisper into mama's ear that if it's Blake, the shoemaker, hide my cigars, because he'll take a handful if he gets a chance. If it's O'Toole, the grocer, hide my whiskey bottle in the basement, because he will drain it dry if he gets his hands on it.

"If it's Vaupel, the druggist, you just sit on your mother's lap until I get home."

He Never Pays Cash

A duck walked into a pharmacy, approached the prescription counter and said to the pharmacist, "I would like to purchase a good over-the-counter cough syrup, please."

The pharmacist acknowledged his request, selected the proper product from his display and inquired, "Will this be a cash sale, sir?"

"No," said the duck, "put it on my bill!"

Many a Pharmacist Drinks to Forget the Woman Who is Driving Him to Drink

A retired pharmacist and his wife were driving down a busy interstate when a highway patrolman pulled them over for speeding. The patrolman approached the car and said, "Sir, do you realize you were doing 65 in a 45 mile speed zone?"

"No, sir," said the pharmacist, "there must be some mistake, I never drive over the speed limit."

The wife spoke up, "Don't you believe him officer. I told him to slow down. He always drive like a maniac." The husband gave his wife a dirty look.

As the patrolman was writing the ticket he said, "Sir, I notice you're not wearing your seat belt. I'll have to write you up for that, too."

"Now wait a minute," answered the pharmacist. "I was wearing my seat belt, I just unfastened it to get at my billfold to get my driver's license."

"Don't you believe that idiot, officer," said the wife. "He never fastens his seat belt. I keep telling him to but he never listens."

The husband turned to his wife and blurted, "Would you please keep your mouth shut!"

The patrolman looked at the wife with sympathy and asked, "Ma'am, is your husband always this abusive?"

"Oh no, officer," said the wife, "only when he's drinking."

Dried Apricots Won't Do It

Little girls like dolls and little boys like soldiers, but after they grow up, the girls go for the soldiers and the boys go for the dolls.

The pharmacist came home after a busy day at the pharmacy and finds his wife in tears.

"What's the problem, dear?" asked the pharmacist.

"It's your son," replied the wife. "He came home from his first day of school and I asked him how it went. He said he ate dried apricots and made love to the girls all day long."

"That's not right," said the pharmacist, "where's the frying pan?"

"My goodness," said the wife, "You can't beat him with the frying pan."

"Who said I was going to beat him?" answered the pharmacist, "I'm going to fry him a steak and fix him some fried potatoes. You can't expect the boy to make love all day on dried apricots."

It Runs In The Family

When it comes to trade relations, most of us would like to.

A pharmacist and his wife from Bismarck, North Dakota, were driving through the great state of South Dakota to visit the Black Hills. He noticed his gas tank was getting low so he pulled into a gas station to get some gas.

The attendant was a talkative individual and said to the pharmacist, "I see by your license plate you're from North Dakota."

The wife, who is hard of hearing said, "What'd he say?"

The pharmacist turned to his wife and shouted "He said he see's we're from North Dakota."

"Oh," answered the wife.

"I've been there," said the attendant. "I really liked the Badlands and Theodore Roosevelt State Park."

The wife asked, "What'd he say?"

The husband shouted in return, "He said he liked the Badlands."

"Oh," said the wife.

The attendant leaned into the car and whispered to the pharmacist, "I met the homeliest woman I ever saw in Bismarck, North Dakota."

The wife asked, "What'd he say?"

The pharmacist yelled in her ear, "He said he thinks he knows your sister."

A Silver Spoon in His Mouth

The penalty for dishonesty is the disgrace of dying rich.

The day that Pepper was born his grandfather set up a prepaid college education for him. When he finished high school he had no idea what he wanted to study but he was determined to make use of his grandfather's gift.

He looked around a bit, talked to some friends, and decided to study pharmacy, even though he had no previous exposure to the profession.

Pepper was a good student and he finished the course. He did his internship, passed the state board examinations and became a registered pharmacist. He was not an overly ambitious person and after a couple of years in the profession he grew tired of the hard work, long hours, and low pay. He decided to go to law school.

He finished this curse, also, and became a pharmacist-lawyer and went to work for a large law firm. Pepper had found his nitch. He loved the big bucks salary of his new profession and he enjoyed cross examining pharmacists on the witness stand.

One day in a heated trial, Pepper dropped dead and presented himself to St. Peter at the Pearly Gate. Pepper was unhappy and he made no bones about it. He protested vigorously and expressed his displeasure to St. Peter. "Why did you call me so early? I was just starting to railroad and I'm a young man," said Pepper.

"Let me check the computer," says St. Peter, "there appears to be something wrong here." St. Peter checked the computer and responded, "According to our records you are 108 years old and it was time for you to go."

"Check that again," demanded Pepper, that's not right. I'm only thirty-two."

"I'll check it again," said St. Peter. He made a thorough check and replied, "The record says you're 108; we base your age on the hours you billed for."

If You Work Hard and Long Enough on a Farm, You Can Make A Fortune -- If You Strike Oil

Lindsay was a successful pharmacist, had made some money, and had taken his pharmacist son into his business. The son was running the business quite well and this freed up Lindsay to look for an outside interest. His brother-in-law had a pig farm and was doing quite well so Lindsay decided to raise some pigs.

He didn't have much knowledge of the pig business, but he lived on a rural acreage and had some extra land. With the help of his brother-in-law he set up a hog operation.

Several months into the operation Lindsay discovered that his pigs were not reproducing. He realized that the success of his venture relied on raising baby pigs, he called his brother-in-law for a consultation.

The brother-in-law ran some tests and delivered the bad new to Lindsay. "All your boars are sterile. At this rate you'll never have any piglets."

"What can I do?" pleaded Lindsay.

"Look," said the brother-in-law, "I've got a dozen vigorous boars and all my females are bred. We'll put my boars to work. You only have twenty-four females and I have a dozen boars, we'll wrap this up in a hurry. Early on Monday morning you load your twenty-four females into your truck and bring them to my place. We'll let them spend the day together and we'll check them at the end of the week. If they're not pregnant, we'll bring them back again the next week."

Lindsay was delighted with this arrangement. On Monday he loaded up his pigs early and delivered them to his brother-in-law's place where they spent the day and were returned home. At the end of the week the brother-in-law checked the females and none were pregnant. "Bring them back again on Monday and we'll try again," said the brother-in-law.

They repeated the process and again on Friday there were no results. "Bring them back on Monday," said the brother-in-law.

Early the next Monday the wife woke the pharmacist and said, "You've got to see this." She led him to the window and he couldn't believe his eyes. The pigs had loaded themselves in the truck and one of them was in the cab honking the horn.

Laugh and the Class Laughs With You, But You Stay After School Alone

My friend, Pharmacist Robensdale, who lost an eye in the Korean War, is known for having a sly sense of humor. He is also known to pull a few pranks now and then. His young son, Charlie, who is in the fifth grade, is said to be following in his father's foot steps.

It was the last week of school, before the summer vacation, and students were getting restless. The teacher knew it was spring fever and the students needed something to keep them interested for this last week.

On Monday the teacher announced, "Each day this week I will ask a question; if anyone in the class can answer the question correctly, the whole class will get the rest of the week off."

The class became immediately excited and the teacher proceeded, "My question for today is, How high is the sky?" No one could answer the question.

On Tuesday the teacher said, "How many inches down in the ground is it to the center of the earth?" No one raised their hand.

On Wednesday, the teacher asked, how many drops of water are in Lake Michigan? On Thursday, she asked how many grains of sand are on the beaches of Florida.

Charlie awoke on Friday morning thoroughly disgusted with the impossible questions the teacher was asking. He stole his father's extra glass eye and took it to school with him.

At the start of class on Friday morning the teacher begins, "Today's question is . . ." Before she can continue, Charlie takes his father's glass eye out of his pocket and rolls it loudly down the isle toward the teacher's desk. The teacher picks it up and says, "OK, who's the funny guy with the glass eye?"

Charlie jumped to his feet and said, "Sammy Davis, Jr! We'll see you in September!"

The Only Thing You Can Save Out Of Your Paycheck These Days Is The Envelope

A pharmacist was visiting the city to attend a meeting. He checked into a motel and went to the restaurant to have dinner. When he was finished, he left the waitress three dimes for a tip.

The next morning before leaving for his meeting, he stopped at the same restaurant to have breakfast.

As he was ushered to a table, he saw that he had the same waitress. "I remember you from last night," said the waitress. "I can tell your fortune from the tip you left me."

"You really can?" said the pharmacist. "Go ahead and do it."

"Well," she said, "since the three dimes were left in a straight line, it shows that you are very neat. The first dime shows that you are very thrifty and the second dime shows that you are a bachelor."

"That's great," said the pharmacist, "But what about the third dime?"

"The third dime shows that your father was also a bachelor."

The More a Preacher Appeases the More He Pleases

Dillard the pharmacist was in church on Sunday Morning. Preacher Smith was in the middle of his sermon when he yelled out, "Anybody who likes sin, stand up!"

Nobody in the congregation stood up, except Dillard.

"Brother Dillard," asked the preacher, "Are you telling me you like sin?"

"Excuse me, Parson," said Dillard, "I thought you said gin."

Some Men Can Take a Drink or Leave it Alone -- For a Few Hours

Old Mr. Gilbert came into the pharmacy to get his prescription refilled. Blake, the pharmacy tech greeted him, "How have you been feeling lately, Mr. Gilbert?"

"I've been under the weather," answered Gilbert. "Doc

Burns gave me some pills to take every day with a little whiskey."

"Are you feeling better than you did?" asked the Tech.

"Not really," said Gilbert, "but I'm two weeks behind on the pills and four weeks ahead on the whiskey."

Miracle Drug

Two ranchers were in the pharmacy on a busy Saturday morning waiting for their prescriptions to be filled.

One rancher addressed the other, "My prize bull cost me five thousand dollars, and when I got him home, I found he was impotent. I called the vet to come out and check him over and he gave me a prescription for a special medicine to give him. I used it for a week and the bull is doing just fine, so I'm having the prescription refilled."

"I have a bull with that problem too," said the other rancher. "What was the medicine the vet prescribed?"

"I don't know," said the first rancher. "But it tastes like licorice."

Strong Drink Can Weaken Character

The prescription shop was on one corner and the City News Stand was on the other. In between the two was Murphy's Bar. The pharmacist had trained his dog to go to the newsstand each morning and fetch the morning newspaper. He would put exactly fifty cents in an envelope and put it under the dog's collar. Then, he would send the dog off to the newsstand.

One morning the pharmacist had only a five-dollar bill, so he placed that in the envelope, knowing that the vendor would send the change back with the dog.

More than an hour passed and the dog did not return,

so the pharmacist went looking for him. As he passed Murphy's bar he saw his dog sitting on a bar stool, drinking beer. Approaching the dog, the pharmacist said, "You've never done this before!"

The dog replied, "I never had the money."

Those Who Live Right Won't Get Left

A pharmacist, a lawyer and a doctor died at the same time and met St. Peter at the golden gate.

St. Peter addressed the group, "I would like to welcome you but before you can be admitted, you must prove your right to enter. What are your qualifications?"

The pharmacist stepped forward and said, "I was a pharmacist for forty years. I filled prescriptions that saved lives and made sick people well."

"That's a noble accomplishment," said St. Peter. "Come right in."

The second fellow stepped forward and said, "I was a lawyer and I defended hundreds of innocent people."

St. Peter responded, "You did quite well, you can come in."

St. Peter turned to the third fellow and asked. "Why should I let you in?"

"I was a doctor," he replied. "I was a managed care professional, I operated an HMO. I helped to keep health care costs down."

St. Peter pondered this response for a minute and replied, "OK, you may come in. But you can only stay three days."

Some Folks Have a Craving For Saving; Others An Urge to Splurge

Pharmacist Fromble was mailing the monthly statements from his Corner Drug Store and noticed customer Pierson had not paid his account for more than a year. Fromble wrote a strong request on the statement demanding payment.

A few days later Fromble received the statement back in the mail and the customer had written, "I will pay you as soon as I repay the money I owe my mother."

Pierson returned the statement with the notation, "I've done more for you than your mother, I've carried you for fifteen months. Pay me first!"

Wisdom is the Ability to Discover Alternatives

I was working in my prescription department on a quiet Saturday afternoon. All of the doctor's offices were closed so it was a slow period and it gave me an opportunity to catch up on a few things.

The telephone rang and a woman's voice inquired, "What time is it?" I looked at my watch and answered, "It's exactly 2:14." She said "Thank you," and hung up.

A short time later the phone rang again and the same voice asked again, "What time is it?" Again I looked at my watch and replied, "It's exactly 2:28." She said, "Thank you," and hung up.

Not long later the phone rang again and the same voice asked, "What time is it?" I was beginning to wonder what was going on and asked, "Didn't you call before?"

"Yes," she responded, "I'm cooking chicken and my timer is broken."

Work Isn't Work if You Enjoy It

I hired a young man to work in the drug store. He was a nice enough fellow and a good worker, but he didn't care much for the drug business. By mutual agreement he decided to seek other employment.

I hadn't seen him for several months and one day he came into the store wearing the uniform of a deputy sheriff. I looked at him and smiled and said, "I see you've got a new job?"

He smiled back and answered, "Yes. What I like about this job is that the customer is always wrong."

It's Not Whether You Win or Lose,
But How You Place the Blame

The pharmacist and the insurance adjustor were walking through the smoldering ruins of the drug store. It was obvious it was a total loss.

"What do you think caused the fire?" inquired the pharmacist.

"It's a clear case of friction," replied the adjustor.

"What do you mean, friction?" asked the pharmacist.

"The fire started by rubbing a $500,000 drug store against a $700,000 insurance policy."

The Cost Of Living Has Gone Up
But Most People Think it's Worth the Price

I was refilling a prescription for a customer who was a stock broker. When I brought up his prescription on the computer I noticed it had gone up in price.

I finished filling the prescription and took it out to the customer and said, "I'm sorry, your prescription went up to $18 today."

He looked at me and responded, "Well, when it goes to $20, SELL."

Never Judge a Book By Its Cover

A pharmaceutical salesman was traveling through the country and a winter storm came up unexpectedly. Realizing he would need to seek shelter, he headed for the nearest farmhouse.

He knocked at the door and explained his situation to the farmer. "You can spend the night," said the farmer, "but you'll have to sleep with my three sons."

"Three sons!" said the salesman, "I must be in the wrong story."

He Who Laughs Last Doesn't Get the Joke

The old pharmacist had worked hard all of his life, operated a successful pharmacy, invested wisely, and made a few bucks. Now he was along in years, was critically ill, and knew that his end was approaching. He called in his lawyer for a conference. "Before I go, I have one more thing to accomplish," said the pharmacist. "I want to become a lawyer. How much did you say that express degree we talked about would cost?"

"It would be about $50,000," said the lawyer. "But why would you want to become a lawyer at this late date?"

"Never mind the reason," said the pharmacist, "take the $50,000 from my account and order the degree." The lawyer did as he is directed, and four days later the old pharmacist got his law degree.

The next day the pharmacist took a turn for the worst and his lawyer was called to his bedside. It was obvious the pharmacist was failing rapidly and that the end is near.

Still curious, the lawyer leaned over to the old pharmacist and said, "I must know, before it is too late. Please tell me why you wanted to become a lawyer before you died?"

In a last desperate effort before he breathed his last, the old pharmacist said, "One less lawyer."

A Joke is Proof That the Good Don't Die Young

Semansky and his wife, Mildred, the pharmacist, had been retired for many years and were discussing their final plans.

"If I die before you, what will you do?" asked Semansky.

Mildred gave the question some thought and replied that she would probably try to reduce expenses. "I would look for a house-sharing situation, probably find two younger single or widowed women who I could live with. What will you do if I die first?" she continued.

Semansky replied, "Probably the same thing."

A Good Round Sum Will Square Things With Most Girls

A young pharmacy graduate applied for a position with a leading super-store pharmacy and presented himself for the interview. As they neared the end of the interview, the company representative asked the new pharmacy graduate, "What starting salary are you expecting?"

"In the area of $100,000 a year, depending on the benefits."

"What would you say to a benefit package like this: a full medical and dental plan, including prescriptions, with no co-pay. six weeks vacation starting the first year, twelve paid holidays, a thirty-six hour week with no nights, weekends or holidays, a company matching retirement fund of up to 50 percent of your salary and a new company convertible sports car lease free every two years?"

The pharmacy grad immediately came to life and said, "Wow! Are you kidding?"

"Certainly," said the interviewer, "but you started it!"

The Mind Makes it First; It's Up to Us to Make it Last

 How many pharmaceutical salesmen does it take to change a light bulb?

Five, one to change the bulb and four to see that the company gets five dollars for every light bulb ever changed anywhere in the world.

If Your Wife Doesn't Treat You as She Should -- Be Thankful

The young pharmacist who had been married just a couple of weeks came home from a busy day at the pharmacy. He was dead tired and laid down on the couch completely exhausted.

His young bride realizes his situation and begins to shower him with sympathy and attention. "I know you have had a busy day, Dear, and I can see that you are tired and hungry. Would you like a nice steak smothered with mushrooms, a fresh vegetable, some french fries and a big slice of apple pie?"

The exhausted pharmacist looked up at his new bride and answered, "Not tonight, Dear, I'm too tired to go out."

All He Ever Gets on a
Silver Platter is Tarnish

Things were running a little tight for Perkins at his community drug store. The year was almost half over and he was still running in the red. It was nearing the end of another month and he was waiting for his bookkeeper's report.

"There's good news today," said the bookkeeper. "That flu epidemic last week finally put us in the black."

"That's great," said Perkins. "Throw out that bottle of red ink and run out and get a bottle of black."

"Oh, we can't do that," said the bookkeeper. "If I went out and bought a bottle of black ink, we would be back in the red again."

It's a Good Idea to See if You're on Firm Ground
Before You Put Your Foot Down

Hildegard was a good pharmacist, she did her work well, related well to the customers, and was a dependable employee. However, she had a problem getting along with management and the other employees. In short, she was a bit of a radical and she liked to rock the boat.

Management decided to establish an employee pension plan, which would add a great benefit for the employees. For the plan to be instituted, it required 100% employee participation; every employee must sign up.

When the vote was taken every employee agreed to sign up, except Hildegard. True to her nature, she found fault with the plan. All of her fellow employees pleaded with Hildegard to sign but still she refused, saying the plan will never pay off.

Finally the store owner called Hildegard into his office

for a private meeting. "Hildegard," he said, "either you sign up for this program or you have worked your last day for this company. Sign up now or you are fired!"

Hildegard took the pen and signed up for the program.

After she had signed the store owner asked, "Now that you have signed up, Hildegard, why did it take you so long to make up your mind?"

Hildegard replied, "You're the first one that explained the program."

I've Never Heard a Joke I Didn't Like

It was the "dirty thirties" and times were tough. A lot of folks were out of work and many took to the railroads as hobos, riding the rails.

Two old friends met on a freight train and one's clothes were so tattered his friend hardly recognized him. "We've got to get you some clean clothes," he said, "those pants look terrible."

"I know," said the friend, "but I have no money, how will I get them?"

"You just have to ask," said the friend. "We'll get off at the next town, find a house that looks prosperous and ask for a pair."

As they walked down the street they found a house with a solid brass mortar and pestle on the door. "A pharmacist lives here," said the friend, "Try this one."

He knocks on the door and a lady answers; the bum

asks if the pharmacist is home. The lady answers, "Yes." So the hobo said, "Would you please ask the pharmacist if he has an old pair of pants that I can have?"

The lady said she couldn't do that so the bum explained, "I don't care about the condition, anything would be better than these."

The lady answered, "That isn't the problem. I'm the pharmacist."

Many a Joke Sounds Too Good To Be New

Siegel was a dedicated pharmacist who spent most of his time running his shop. He had little outside interests and his vices were few.

He did, however, belong to a poker club, made up of six other pharmacists who had been friends for years and meet once a month.

His wife didn't care much for gambling or for his "night out with the boys." However, since it was just once a month, she put up with it. Her pet peeve was that he made so much noise coming home late in the evening that he always woke her up and she had difficulty getting back to sleep.

One night he came home way after midnight and decided not to wake her up. He undressed in the living room and tiptoed nude into the bedroom. Much to his surprise he found his wife sitting up in bed reading.

She looked up from her book and said, "Good Lord, did you lose everything?"

If It's Laughter You're After . . .

Ribble and his wife had been working late at the pharmacy doing their quarterly reports. They were tired but decided to stop at their favorite lounge for a nightcap.

The lounge was crowded so they took a seat at the bar, next to an old drunk who looked as if he had been there for most of the day.

All of a sudden the drunk lets out a thunderous belch that startled everyone in the bar. Ribble is dismayed and says to the drunk, "How dare you belch in front of my wife?"

The drunk looks up at Ribble and says, "I'm sorry, buddy, I didn't know it was her turn!"

Life is Wonderful; Without it You'd be Dead

Old Dennison is an eighty-five year old widowed pharmacist who has taken up with a petite twenty-two year old redhead. After a short time he calls his children and grandchildren together and announces that he is about to get married. The family is astounded, and the oldest son took the elderly gentleman aside for a consultation.

"Father," he said, "how can you do something so outrageous? You are over eighty-five years old and she is only twenty-two. Do you realize this could be fatal?"

The old pharmacist smiled and replied, "If she dies, she dies!"

One of These Days Is None of These Days

Devaney is a bachelor pharmacist who has a reputation for being a bit of a playboy and for having an eye for the ladies. He also owns a very successful pharmacy, is a good businessman, and enjoys the finer things in life.

A major pharmaceutical company sponsored a continuing education program in the city and invited all the area pharmacists to attend. The continuing education session was followed by a cocktail hour and a fine sit-down dinner.

During the education session Devaney spotted a very attractive young lady pharmacist who has just moved to the area and has taken a position as a pharmacist at an area hospital. He makes a mental note to seek her out during the cocktail hour.

During the cocktail hour, he sidles up to her, introduces himself, and inquires, "Can I get you another drink?"

She takes a sip from her drink and says, "That'll be the day."

"How about if I sit next to you at dinner?" he further inquired.

She took a sip from her drink and replied, "That'll be the day."

"Well then," he continued, "how about if after dinner we get into my Cadillac convertible and I drive you over and show you my professional pharmacy that fills four hundred prescriptions a day and is all paid for?"

She took another sip from her drink and replied, "This will be the day."

The One Who Laughs Last Usually Has a Tooth Missing

This newly graduated pharmacy technician is walking down the street when she sees a man lying face down in the gutter.

She remembered her first-aid course and rushed over to him, rolled him over on his back, and begins to give him mouth-to-mouth resuscitation.

The guy suddenly sits up straight and says, "I don't know what you have in mind, Lady, but could you give me a few minutes to finish cleaning out the drain?"

The Best Way to Cure Insomnia Is to Get Lots of Sleep

All of the other pharmacists were worried about Truman. His wife had divorced him and the past month appeared to have been hard on him. He was tired all the time, was not very alert, and really looked run down.

One of his pharmacist friends approached him and said, "Truman, you've got to pull yourself together. You've got to get over this and go on to something else. What's your biggest problem?"

"I'm not sleeping at night," answered Truman.

"Why don't you try counting sheep?" asked the friend.

"I'm too busy counting my lucky stars."

There's Many a Slip 'twixt Editor and Contributor

Pharmacist Perry King decided to take up skydiving. After a couple of years he became quite proficient at the sport and decided to become an instructor. His success as an instructor continued to the point that he decided to write a book on the subject.

He completed the book and had a thousand copies published which quickly sold out.

No sooner was the last copy sold when Perry discovered a serious typographical error. The error was so serious, in fact, that he was forced to write a notice of retraction. It was fortunate that Perry had the name and address of every purchaser of the book so he sent this letter to each purchaser:

"I regret to inform you that there is a typographical error on page 81 of my book, *How To Skydive In Ten Easy Lessons*. In the second paragraph where it reads, "Count to ten and state your zip code," should read, "Count to ten and pull the rip cord." I regret any inconvenience this error may have caused."

Many A Joke Sounds Too Good To Be New

The Red River overflowed in this little Minnesota town and caused a major flood. A man and his wife were sitting on the roof of their house watching different items floating along the water. They noticed a derby hat floating by but pretty soon it turns around and comes by in the other direction. Then it turns again and goes back up stream.

The wife said, "Do you see that derby? First it heads up stream, then it turns around and heads down. Then it turns around and heads up stream again, then it comes back."

The husband replied, "That's our next door neighbor, Morgan, the druggist. He said he was going to cut his grass today come hell or high water."

Goosed

"He writes so well it makes me want to put my quill back in my goose."
_ Fred Allen

Most Poets Will Tell You:
Rhyme Doesn't Pay

"I retired in 1987, and when you retire you get the gold watch, and then what? You die. Unless, of course,

111

you write a best-selling book. Everyone should do that ; find your own voice and dance your own dance! Just get that book out there.

_ Frank McCourt

Angela's Ashes

Loser

Whoever it was that said, "It's not whether you win or lose that counts," probably lost.

Did You Ever Know an Idle Rumor That Remained Idle?

A pharmacist died and went to heaven and met St. Peter at the Golden Gate. St. Peter welcomed him and said, "You certainly deserve to be here but we're running out of space. Do you see that hill over there that we have reserved for pharmacists? It's full, there isn't a space left."

"Give me a week to start a rumor," said the pharmacist. "I think I can remedy that situation." The pharmacist went to the heavenly bulletin board and posted this notice: Wal-mart is coming to heaven. As the rumor spread the gates of heaven opened and there was a mass exodus.

St. Peter said to the pharmacist, "There's plenty of room now, you can move right in."

"I've changed my mind," said the pharmacist. "There might be some truth to that rumor!"

I've Hated Dogs Ever Since I Went to a Masquerade Ball as a Lamp Post

A pharmaceutical sales representative was traveling his rural territory and stopped at a remote country store to get some gas. After he served himself he went into the store to pay his bill. He glanced to the back of the store and saw five men playing poker with a St. Bernard dog.

He walked over to the table and stood and watched the game for a while. The dog drew two cards, raised the bet, won the pot and raked in the chips.

"That's amazing," said the salesman. "I've never seen such a smart dog in all my life."

One of the guys looked up and said, "He ain't so smart. Everytime he gets a good hand, he wags his tail."

My Ear Is Ringing. Pardon Me While I Answer It

A man walked into a pharmacy with a banana in each of his ears. He approached the prescription counter and

the pharmacist looked at him and said, "Excuse me, sir, you have bananas in your ears!"

The man looked at the pharmacist with a puzzled look and said, "What did you say?"

The pharmacist repeated, "You have bananas in your ears."

The man answered. "I'm sorry, I can't hear a word you're saying. I have bananas in my ears."

113

Some People Stand on the Promise; Others Just Sit on the Promiser

Sake managed a neighborhood pharmacy for a pharmacist who owned a small chain of five stores. One day the owner showed up for a surprise visit and found a young man sitting lazily in the corner.

The owner was visibly upset and angrily asked the young man, "Just how much are you being paid a week?"

"Three hundred bucks," replied the young man.

Taking out his billfold and removing some cash, the owner handed the young man some cash and said "Here's a week's pay. Now get out of here and don't come back."

Turning to Sake the owner asked, "How long has that lazy bum been working here anyway?"

"He doesn't work here," said Sake. "He works for the freight company and just delivered our order. He was waiting for me to sign the freight bill."

To Err is Human but to Admit it is Not

Slaten and Gore were partners in a busy pharmacy. Slaten became suddenly ill and was on his death bed.

Gore was at his bedside and suddenly Slaten rose up and said to his partner, "I know I'm dying and I have a confession to make. I stole fifty thousand dollars from our office safe. I'm the one who told your wife about your affair with the girl at the cosmetic counter, and I've been running my personal household expenses through the drug store."

"That's OK," said Gore. "I poisoned you."

Advice is Like a Laxative -- Easy to Take But Hard to Predict the Outcome

An elderly gentleman stepped off the curb against a red light at a busy intersection and was hit by a car.

Durall, the pharmacist, came upon the scene and stopped to see if he could render first aid. A little old lady in the crowd that gathered screamed, "Give the poor fellow a drink of whiskey."

Another person shouted, "Stand back and give him some air."

Durall was assessing the damages and the little old lady said again, "Give him a drink of whiskey!"

Someone else shouted, "Call an ambulance."

Again the little old lady shouted, "Give him a drink of whiskey!"

Suddenly the victim sat up and yelled, "Would all of you please shut up and listen to the little old lady!"

If You Have an Excuse, Don't Use It

Pharmacist Lomardi and his wife were attending the state pharmacists convention and checked into a motel opposite the railroad station. The next morning Lomardi got up early to attend a continuing education session and left his wife in bed.

About an hour later a train passed, and the vibrations knock Lombardi's wife out of bed. She got back in bed and a few minutes later another train passed, and again the vibration knocks her out of bed. Ten minutes later the same thing happened.

This time Mrs. Lombardi called the motel manager

and registered a complaint.

"I don't believe that can happen," said the manager. "We've never had a complaint like that before."

"Come up and see for yourself," said Mrs. Lombardi.

The manager went to the room and Mrs. Lombardi said, "I'm lying in the bed and everytime a train passes the vibration knocks me out of bed. Lie down on the bed and see for yourself."

The manager is lying on the bed about five minutes when her husband walks in the door and says to the manager, "What the hell are you doing in my bed?"

The manager answered, "Would you believe I'm waiting for a train?"

The Table-Tennis Match

The College of Pharmacy had a very active Kappa Psi fraternity on the campus of the university. The fraternity took an active part in campus activities and supported many community projects. As a result of the cooperative efforts of all the members, the fraternity was held in high esteem on the campus and in the community.

The fraternity also took an active role in sports activities. Its long suit was table tennis, and they won the college championship four years in a row.

In a very competitive championship match, one of the Kappa Psi players caught a slammed ball in his mouth and swallowed it. An ambulance delivered him to the local hospital where emergency surgery was performed. Complications developed during the surgery and the operation lasted several hours.

When the player came out of the anesthetic, he was in his room and the surgeon was standing beside him. As the patient assessed his condition, he thanked the doctor for pulling him through, but questioned, "Why do

116

I have 12 incisions across my stomach?"

The doctor cocked his head, raised his palms, and replied, "That's the way the old ball bounces."

It's True That Gifts to Charity are Deductible From Your Income Tax; The Trouble is, They Also are Deductible From Your Income

The community was having a fund drive for charity, and the chairman took on the chore of calling on the high rollers. The objective was to get the wealthy businessmen to make a sizeable donation. The chairman made an appointment to call on Rossler, the pharmacist, to solicit a healthy donation.

"You are one of the leading businessmen in our community," said the chairman, "Yet you have never contributed to our cause. Don't you feel you should contribute this year?"

"Do you realize that I have two children in pharmacy school?" said the pharmacist. "Do you know that my sister's husband left her alone with six children to look after? Are you aware that my brother was severely wounded in the war and has no means of support? Since I don't give them a dime, what makes you think I will donate to your fund?"

Television Isn't so Bad if You Don't Turn it On

The nurse told the patient, "There's absolutely no cause for worry. The doctor has seen an operation exactly like yours on TV."

Testimonial for a Hair Restorer:

Before I used your restorer, I had three bald patches. Now I have one.

The King of Mean

I had been a registered pharmacist for a couple of years when I took a job in a small-town pharmacy. The prescription department was very busy, and the town had a busy hospital and a large number of physicians for its size. It was recognized as the area medical center.

A block up the street was the office of Dr. Steffenson. Old Steffenson had been around for years. He was a pretty fair mechanic, but mean as sin.

Back in those days, some pharmacists were known to do a little "counter prescribing," and old Steffenson had a special dislike for pharmacists. I was no exception. My longest days were those that started out by getting chewed out by old Steffenson.

One day, a friend of mine came into the pharmacy with a strange skin rash. He had been on a camping trip with his son, so I knew he had encountered a strange weed that did not agree with him.

Mean as he was, old Steffenson was pretty good on skin rashes, so I suggested my friend see him. As Steffenson examined the patient, he asked, "Did you see any other doctor before you came to see me?"

"No," said my friend. "I went to see the young pharmacist at the corner drug store."

The infuriated Steffenson really hit the roof, and said, "All pharmacists are stupid and that one especially so. A little bit of knowledge is dangerous. What did that idiot tell you?"

My friend was astounded and said, "Why, he told me to come and see you."

A Bill Collector Doesn't Believe in Putting Off Until Tomorrow What Can be Dunned Today

Vernon owned a neighborhood pharmacy and a strike at the area's leading employer put his accounts receivable into a negative cash flow situation. As a result, he was unable to pay his bills promptly. One of his suppliers refused to ship his order until his past due account was brought up to date.

Vernon sent them the following letter: "Sir, my stenographer, being a lady, cannot type what I think of you. I, being a gentleman, won't dictate it. But you, being neither, will know what I mean."

MIlions of Americans Aren't Working but Thank Heaven They Have Jobs

The following notice appeared on the bulletin board of a small chain pharmacy: "We are asking that somewhere between starting and quitting time - without infringing on lunchtime, coffee breaks, rest periods, ticket selling and vacation planning -- each employee find some time that can be used for what is know as Work Break. We believe this will be an aid to steady employment and regular paychecks, and we hope that each employee will give it a fair trial."

Selling is Easy but Only if You Work Hard at It

Pharmaceutical salesman on his first day on the job - "I got two orders - 'Get out' and 'Stay out'."

When a Physician Makes His Mark, It's Usually Illegible

A local physician came into the pharmacy and wrote a prescription for a controlled substance. "The patient will be by to pick it up," said the doctor.

The pharmacist looked at the prescription and reminded the physician that he didn't dot the "i" in his signature.

"Could you do that for me?" asked the doctor.

"Sorry," said the pharmacist, "It must be in your handwriting!"

Every Estimate Ought to Include an Estimate of How Much More it Will be Than the Estimate

The customer had a serious case of constipation and stopped in at the pharmacy to explain his problem. "Can you give me something that will bring me some relief?" asked the customer.

"I'm sure I can," said the pharmacist as he took out a graduate and a bottle of medicine. "Tell me," said the pharmacist, "how tall are you and how much do you weigh?"

"I'm five foot eight," replied the customer, "and I weigh 146 pounds."

The pharmacist started to pour the medicine into the graduate and continues, 'How far are you from home?"

"Two miles," answered the customer.

The pharmacist added to the graduate and asked, "Do you have an inside toilet or an outside toilet?"

The patient relied, "Outside."

The pharmacist added to the graduate and continued, "How many steps is it from the back door of your house to the outhouse?"

"It's thirty-two steps," replied the customer.

The pharmacist added to the graduate, handed it to the customer and said, "Drink this down and head for home!" The customer did as he was instructed.

Three days later the customer returned to the pharmacy. The pharmacist recognized him at once and asked, "How did it work?"

"Actually, quite well," said the customer. "In fact, you only missed it by three steps. I think I could have made it if I hadn't hit the clothes line!"

The Chief Cause of All Divorces Is Matrimony

The retired pharmacist and her husband were before the judge seeking a divorce. "You're 92," said the judge, "your husband is 94. You've been married 72 years. Why would you want a divorce now?"

The pharmacist replied, "We've been waiting for the children to die!"

Work Is a Fine Thing If It Doesn't Take Up Too Much of Your Spare Time

The pharmacist answered his grumbling wife, "I'm relaxing in my favorite chair on Sunday, reading the newspaper, watching a ball game on TV, and listening to another on the radio, drinking beer, eating a snack, and  scratching the dog with my foot, and you have the nerve to accuse me of just sitting there doing nothing!"

All Babies Are Subject To Change Without Notice

I asked my friend, Pruitt, to tell me the funniest thing that ever happened to him as a pharmacist. He related this event:

A young bride approached his prescription counter and inquired, "I've been reading those advertisements about baby vitamin drops. Is it true they will make the baby bigger and stronger?"

Pruitt assured her that medical research had revealed that vitamin formulas were an essential ingredient for proper health and growth of a child.

"I just wanted to be sure," replied the customer. "I'll take a bottle." She made her purchase and left the store. In just a few minutes she was back again and called the pharmacist to the consultation area.

"I forgot to ask you," she whispered. "Who takes these vitamins -- me or my husband?"

Watch Out for the Girl Who Is Pretty as a Picture -- You May Be the Man She's Out to Frame

My friend, Ralph, had a pharmacy in a resort area on the edge of a beautiful lake. The lake had numerous inlets that were remote and secluded with beautiful sandy beaches that gave a lot of privacy. The lake attracted visitors by the thousands.

Taking advantage of this situation, Ralph invested in a one hour photo finishing service and developed a land office business.

A big event had taken place at a nursing home in the city. A very popular lady who was well known as a community leader, had reached her 100th birthday and a citywide community event was planned. Needless to say, this was a real shot in the arm to Ralph's one hour photo finishing business.

At the same time it seems that a young woman and her boyfriend had planned a romantic weekend on the beach. The frolicking lover presented their film for developing at the same time as the family of the elderly community leader. While the young couple wanted their pictures finished immediately, the elderly lady's family opted for the slower, regular service.

At the proper time, the young couple called for their photos and immediately left the pharmacy. The young lady returned a short time later and very unhappily displayed her displeasure. She went to Ralph, tossed the photo envelope on the counter and said, "These are not my pictures!"

Ralph examined the photos and could see at once that they were of the elderly lady's community event. Birthday cake and balloons, community leaders and crazy hats were the subject of every photo. It was evident that an error had been made in packaging the photos.

Ralph acknowledged that an error had been made and apologized profusely to the young woman. He went on to explain that there was little he could do until the other party returned the pictures that they had received.

About three days later a little old lady approached Ralph with a smirk on her face and photo finishing envelope in her hand. "I think I got someone else's photos," she said with a smile.

Ralph opened the package to examine the photos. Here was the young woman and her boyfriend frolicking on the beach in various poses in the suits that nature had provided them.

The little old lady grinned at Ralph and smiled, "I could never be a nudist. I always spill coffee in my lap!"

It's Always Difficult to Tell a Woman's Age -- At Least, for Her

The pharmacist was interviewing a lady for the position of pharmacy tech and sat across the desk from her as she filled out the job application form. When she came to the space for age, she hesitated for a long time.

The pharmacist looked at her with a smile and said, "The longer you wait, the worse it gets."

He Has a Heart of Gold -- Yellow and Hard

Gasper had a reputation for being a bit of a hard nose when it came to parting with a buck. He also prided himself in being a bit of a diplomat when it came to side stepping a request for a donation.

The community concert association was holding a special concert to raise funds for the year's operating expenses. The chairman of the ticket committee called on Gasper at his pharmacy to sell him a ticket.

"I'm sorry, but I won't be able to attend the concert," said Gasper. "It's a most worthy cause, and I assure you, I will be with you in spirit."

"Fine," said the ticked chairman. "Now where would like your spirit to sit? The tickets are $5 and $10."

Gasper responded, "I'll take a $10 ticket."

I Never Drink Unless I'm Alone or with Somebody

Dempsey was a retired pharmacist, so it goes without saying that he did not have a lot of money. He walked into a pub and grabbed a seat at the bar. "What can I get for you?" asked the bartender.

"Whiskey," replied Dempsey. The bartender set him up and since business was brisk, continued working.

Soon he was back and said to Dempsey, "That will be $3."

"Oh no!" said Dempsey. "You asked me what I wanted and I told you and you gave it to me!"

The bartender was taken by surprise, stepped back and looked down the bar at other customers. "He's right," explained one of the customers. "I'm a lawyer and he has every right to refuse to pay under these circumstances." The bartender was furious and orders Dempsey out of his bar.

A few minutes later, the bartender found Dempsey back at the bar. He looked at Dempsey and said, "Didn't I just run you out of here?"

"It couldn't have been me," said Dempsey. "There must be some mistake."

"If that is so," said the bartender, "you must have a double!"

"Thank you," said Dempsey, "and one for my lawyer friend, too!"

Humor in Pharmacy

Cliff Thomas

Words of Wisdom for Pharmacists

♦ Never do card tricks for the group that you play poker with.

♦ The problem with the gene pool is that there is no lifeguard.

♦ Two wrongs are only the beginning.

♦ A conscience is what hurts when all your other parts feel so good.

♦ The sooner you fall behind, the more time you'll have to catch up.

♦ A clear conscience is usually the sign of a bad memory.

♦ Don't sweat petty things . . . or pet sweaty things.

♦ If you must choose between two evils, pick the one you've never tried before.

♦ A fool and his money are soon partying.

♦ A pharmacist knows she's getting old when she wakes up with the morning-after feeling, and she didn't do anything the night before.

♦ Money doesn't bring the pharmacist happiness, but it enables them to look for it in more places.

127

♦ A pharmacist who can smile when things go wrong has found someone to blame it on.

♦ Money isn't everything; there are credit cards, money orders, and travelers checks.

♦ Misers aren't much fun to live with, but they make great ancestors.

♦ When you see the handwriting on the wall you can bet you're in a public restroom.

♦ Be careful what rut you choose. You may be in it the rest of your life.

♦ The severity of the itch is proportional to the reach.

♦ Reading Letters to the Editor is like eating a bar of chocolate. You never know when you're going to run into the nuts.

♦ A pharmacist shouldn't take life too seriously -- it's not permanent.

♦ Junk is something you throw away three weeks before you need it.

♦ Opportunities always look bigger going than coming.

♦ A pharmacist has reached middle age when she is cautioned to slow down by her doctor rather than the police.

♦ Experience is a wonderful thing. It enables you to recognize a mistake when you make it again.

♦ You know the pharmacist is getting older when he stops buying green bananas.

♦ If you think nobody cares about you, try missing a couple of payments.

♦ Borrow money from pessimists ... they don't expect to get it back.

♦ Hard work pays off in the future. Laziness pays off now.

♦ Eagles may soar, but skunks aren't sucked into jet engines.

♦ A bird in the hand can be an awful mess.

♦ She told him he looked like a million and she meant every year of it.

♦ Advice is something that most people take for a cold.

♦ Tip for doctors: In case of amnesia, collect the fee in advance.

♦ Work is a fine thing if it doesn't take up too much of your spare time.

♦ Give a woman an inch and she thinks she's a ruler.

♦ Every pharmacist has a photographic memory, some just don't have film.

♦ The Energizer Bunny was arrested -- charged with battery.

♦ The Ode of the Pharmacist -- If you can't convince them, confuse them.

♦ When you see a pharmacist in his underwear with a spent look on his face, he's just finished running 26 miles -- or just finished paying his taxes.

♦ Considering all the White House sex scandals, maybe our national symbol should be changed from an eagle to a rabbit.

♦ The trouble with life is, by the time you can read a girl like a book, your library card has expired.

♦ As we grow older year by year, the pharmacist always mourns; the less we feel our oats, the more we feel our corns.

♦ You're getting old when you don't care where your wife goes, just so you don't have to go along.

Short Snorts

Humor in Pharmacy

When You Are Wrong, No One Forgets

A family practice physician and his friend the pharmacist were having coffee in the hospital coffee shop. "I have a very interesting case," said the physician, "but the internist and I are having a problem agreeing on the diagnosis. This also happened the last time he was called in for a consultation, but I stood my ground."

"What happened?" inquired the pharmacist.

The physician replied, "The autopsy proved me right!"

I Never Heard a Joke I Didn't Like

The patient handed the pharmacist a handful of prescriptions and made the comment, "I don't know about this doctor."

"What is the problem?" asked the pharmacist.

"Well," said the patient, "when I asked the doctor how I should take these pills, he wrote out the instructions for me. It says that I should take the red pills with two full glasses of water when I get up in the morning, take the blue pills with two full glasses of water after lunch and take the green pill with two full glasses of water at bedtime."

"Those instructions sound plain enough to me," said the pharmacist, "why are you questioning this?"

"I asked the doctor, 'What is my problem?,' and he said, 'You're not drinking enough water.'"

Good News/Bad news

Doctor to patient: I have good news and I have bad news. The good news is that you are not a hypochondriac.

You Can't Win 'em All

A computer salesman had been selling computer programs to pharmacies for a number of years. Unexpectedly he had a heart attack and met St. Peter at the Golden Gate.

St. Peter welcomed the salesman, and said he had led an exemplary life. Since they had openings in either place, he could take his choice, heaven or hell.

First, St. Peter showed the salesman heaven. People were dressed in white, playing harps and floating all over the place. "This looks very dull to me," said the salesman, "let me take a look at hell."

St. Peter gave him a look at hell. People were dancing, eating good food, drinking wine, and having a great time. "I'll take hell," said the salesman.

He entered the gates of hell and was immediately set upon by a large group of demons who poked him with pitchforks.

As Satan walked past, the salesman shouted, "Hey, where are all the parties I saw going on?"

"Ah," Satan replied, "you must have seen our demo."

You Expect Results; You Get Consequences

A self-righteous preacher reprimanded a pharmacist because he cussed and drank, "I'm over 60 years old and I've never cussed or drank."

Thepharmacist replied, "Yeah, and you've never owned a drug store, either."

A Frog in Hand ...

Two women were out for a walk and came upon a frog who said, "Pick me up and kiss me and I'll turn back into a hard working pharmacist."

The first woman picked up the frog and put him in her purse.

The second woman asked, "Why not kiss him?"

The first replied, "Hard working pharmacists are a dime a dozen -- but a talking frog -- now, that's something!"

There Are a Lot of Hot Arguments Over 'Cold Cash'

A pharmacist died, went to heaven, and met God. In the discussion, God granted the pharmacist one question. The pharmacist asked, "Will the third party payment program ever get to the point where the pharmacist will be able to make a buck?"

"I have good news and bad news," God replied. "The good new is, this will come to pass. But the bad news is, not in my lifetime."

Of Two Evils, Choose Neither

Pharmacist Fellows was not feeling well, so his wife called his doctor's office to make an appointment.

"I'm sorry," said the receptionist, "but we're very busy. We can't fit him in for at least two weeks."

"He could be dead by then," replied the pharmacist's wife.

"That's not a problem." said the receptionist, "Just give us a call and we'll cancel the appointment."

135

You Never Can Tell: Every Now and Then the Best Man Wins

A pharmaceutical salesman is in the hospital cafeteria. He spots a Coke machine and puts in a coin, out pops a Coke.

The rep looks amazed and runs away to get more coins. He returns and starts feeding the machine madly and of course the machine keeps feeding out drinks.

The director of nurses walks up behind the pharmaceutical sales representative and watches his antics for a few minutes before stopping him and asking if she could have a go at a Coke.

The rep looks at the nursing director in amazement and says, "Can't you see I'm winning?"

It Isn't the Travel That's Broadening; It's All That Rich Foreign Food

Two pharmacist from the old country immigrated to America and were working the streets of New York City.

The first pharmacist said, "I hear that the occupants of this country actually eat dogs."

"That seems odd," said the second pharmacist, "but if we are to live in America, we must do as the American's do."

The first pharmacist nodded in agreement and pointed to a hot dog vendor, and they both approach him. "Two dogs, please," said the first pharmacist.

With a smile the vendor dispensed two hot dogs, each wrapped in foil.

The pharmacists hurried to a bench and began to unwrap the "dogs."

The first pharmacist unwrapped his and, staring at

136

it for a moment, leaned over to the other pharmacist and whispered cautiously, "What part did you get?"

You Never See Angels With Beards Because Men Who Get to Heaven Make it Only by a Close Shave

A pharmacist, a doctor, and a lawyer all died and went to heaven. St. Peter met them at the Golden Gate, but he was having a bad day because heaven is getting over-crowded. He informed them that there would be a test to get into heaven.

To the pharmacist, he said, "What was the name of the ship that crashed into the iceberg and sank with all its passengers?"

The pharmacist thought for a minute and replied, "That was the Titanic." St. Peter opened the gate and let the pharmacist in.

Next, St. Peter turned to the doctor, and realizing he has little space left, decided to make the question harder. "How many people died on the ship?" asked St. Peter.

"1,228," replied the doctor.

"That's exactly right," exclaimed St. Peter, "come right in."

St. Peter then turned to the lawyer and said, "Name them!"

You Can Always Tell a Pharmacist But You Have to Tell Him Twice

A guy in a bar leaned over to the guy next to him and said, "Wanna hear a real dirty joke about a corner druggist?"

The guy next to him replied, "Before you tell me that joke you should know something. I'm six foot tall, 200 pounds and I'm a pharmacist. The guy sitting next to me is six foot two, 225 pounds and he's a pharmacist. The fellow next to him is six foot five, 250 pounds and he's a pharmacist. Do you still want to tell that joke?"

The first guy said, "Nah, I don't want to have to explain it three times."

Pharmacist-Tech Banter

Humor in Pharmacy

Pharmacist: Why do you think diarrhea is hereditary?
Pharmacy Tech: Because it runs in your jeans.

Pharmacy Tech: How many doctors does it take
to screw in a light bulb?
Pharmacist: That depends on whether or not the light bulb
has a health insurance policy.

Pharmacy Tech: Why did you leave your girl friend's house
so early?
Pharmacist: Well, we were sitting on the sofa and she turned
off the light. I can take a hint.

Pharmacist: Why aren't you going out with Bill Jones
anymore?
Pharmacy Tech: Well, he's not too bright and he's not much
to look at, and he got married to Ann Smith.

Pharmacist: What is the difference between God and a
doctor?
Pharmacy Tech: God doesn't think he's a doctor.

Pharmacist: How do you hide a $100 bill from a surgeon.
Pharmacy Tech: Put it under his charts.

Pharmacist: Is Mable still dating that x-ray technician?
Pharmacy Tech: Yes, and I can't understand why. He has no
personality and he's as ugly as sin.
Pharmacist: She must see something in him that others
can't see.

Pharmacy Tech: I saw the doctor you advised me to see.
Pharmacist: What did he say?

Pharmacy Tech: He made me pay in advance.

Pharmacist: I see the doctor got you back on your feet.
Pharmacy Tech: You're right! I had to sell my car to pay his bill.

Pharmacy Tech: There's one advantage to being poor.
Pharmacist: What's that?
Pharmacy Tech: The doctor will cure you much faster.

Pharmacy Tech: What's the difference between a general practitioner and a specialist?
Pharmacist: The specialist has a smaller practice and a bigger boat.

Pharmacy Tech: When the doctor did my operation, I think he left a sponge in me.
Pharmacist: Why do you think that? Are you having any pain?
Pharmacy Tech: No, but I'm thirsty all the time.

Pharmacy Tech: He says he has a ringing in his ears.
Pharmacist: Tell him not to answer it.

Pharmacist: What are you taking for your cold?
Pharmacy Tech: What will you give me?

Pharmacy Tech: My doctor friend refuses to come out to my farm any more.
Pharmacist: Why is that?
Pharmacy Tech: He said my ducks insulted him.

Pharmacy Tech: I have discovered that talk is not cheap.
Pharmacist: How did you discover that?

Pharmacy Tech: I started talking to a psychiatrist.

Pharmacist: Are you doing anything this evening?
Pharmacy Tech: Nothing at all.
Pharmacist: Good. Then you should be able to be on time tomorrow morning.

Pharmacist: How is your wife doing on her reducing diet?
Pharmacy Tech: Just great. She disappeared last week.

Pharmacist: Why is it that you fat people are always so good natured?
Pharmacy Tech: We have to be, we can neither fight nor run.

Pharmacist: Is your wife a good cook?
Pharmacy Tech: When my wife takes a TV dinner out of the oven and removes the aluminium foil, she's tossing out the best part.

Pharmacist: Have you lost your sense of humor? You don't laugh at our boss's jokes any more.
Pharmacy Tech: I don't have to laugh at them any more. I'm quitting Friday.

Pharmacy Tech: I don't like the looks of the new bookkeeper you hired. She's the homeliest woman I ever saw. Besides, she limps and she stutters.
Pharmacist: That's the reason I hired her. If she steals, she'll be easier to identify.

Pharmacy Tech: Could you lend me $50?
Pharmacist: Sorry, I can't. I made a deal with the bank. If they don't fill any prescriptions and I won't lend any money.

Pharmacist: I see that 35-year-old Mrs. Cochran presented her 85-year-old husband with a set of twins. What do you think of that?
Pharmacy Tech: I'm thinking the same thing you're thinking.

Pharmacy Tech: Why do you always call them "wonder drugs?"
Pharmacist: Because I wonder if patients will be able to afford them.

Pharmacist: Why is that patient jumping up and down like that?
Pharmacy Tech: He took his medicine and didn't shake the bottle.

Pharmacy Tech: What is a miracle drug anyway?
Pharmacist: One that you can get kids to take without screaming their heads off.

Pharmacy Tech: What do you give a girl who has everything?
Pharmacist: Penicillin.

Pharmacy Tech: Are there any contra-indications for this new miracle drug?
Pharmacist: Yes, you have to be in perfect health to take it.

Pharmacy Tech: This is a very strong laxative. What shall I tell the patient?
Pharmacist: Tell him you're giving him his change in dimes.

Pharmacy Tech: Why is everyone so quiet in a drug store?

Pharmacist: They don't want to wake up the sleeping pills.

Pharmacy Tech: Why are you so sure that just one bottle of these pills will cure him?
Pharmacist: Because nobody has ever come back for a second bottle.

Pharmacy Tech: What do you mean by a rumor?
Pharmacist: That's something that goes in one ear and in the other.

Pharmacy Tech: Your competitor is a great druggist, isn't he?
Pharmacist: He puts too much salt in his chicken salad.

Pharmacist: Why did he say he wanted his wife's prescription for sleeping pills refilled?
Pharmacy Tech: He said she woke up again.

Pharmacist: I understand your uncle lost his glasses.
Pharmacy Tech: Yes, now he has to drink from the bottle.

Pharmacy Tech: Why are you always so kind to your mother-in-law?
Pharmacist: Because baby-sitters are expensive.

Pharmacist: Why did you quit going out with that perfect 36?
Pharmacy Tech: My wife came in with a loaded .45.

Pharmacy Tech: What does it take for a druggist to be able to operate a really good lunch counter?
Pharmacist: He has to really know his onions.

Pharmacy Tech: When I was first married I'd come home from a hard day's work at the pharmacy; I would be happily met. My dog would run around barking and my wife would bring my slippers. Now things have changed. My dog brings my slippers and my wife barks at me.
Pharmacist: You have nothing to complain about, you're still getting the same service.

Pharmacy Tech: That patient you had me make change for is almost blind.
Pharmacist: I told you he didn't look good.

Pharmacist: You said you bought a horse; but why did you buy only one spur?
Pharmacy Tech: I figured that if I got one side of the horse to go, the other would follow.

Pharmacy Tech: Do you have any part-time jobs?
Pharmacist: Yes, but right now they are all filled with full-time people.

Pharmacy Tech: Could I have this afternoon off to attend my grandmother's funeral?
Pharmacist: Of course you can, in fact, why don't I go with you?

Pharmacist: Why do you always answer a question with a question?
Pharmacy Tech: Do I?

Pharmacist: Are you happy in your job?
Pharmacy Tech: I never knew what real happiness was until I started working here - but then, it was too late.

Pharmacy Tech: The guy who delivers our freight has

all kinds of money.
Pharmacist: Is he rich?
Pharmacy Tech: No, he's a coin collector.

Pharmacist: If you do good work we will give you a raise.
Pharmacy Tech: I knew there would be a catch to it.

Pharmacist: Where are you going on your vacation this year?
Pharmacy Tech: To the bank for a loan.

Pharmacist: I'll start you at $7.50 an hour, for the first six months, then $10.00 an hour after that. Do you want this job?
Pharmacy Tech: Sure, I'll be back in six months.

Pharmacy Tech: I don't usually mix business with pleasure but today I will.
Pharmacist: How will you do that?
Pharmacy Tech: I quit.

Pharmacist: How was your vacation?
Pharmacy Tech: It was great, but it's nice to be back at work, I needed the rest.

Pharmacist: Whom shall we notify in case of an emergency?
Pharmacy Tech: A doctor.

Pharmacy Tech: We're taking up a collection for a going away gift for the boss.
Pharmacist: I didn't know he planned to leave.
Pharmacy Tech: He isn't, but we figured it was worth a try.

Pharmacy Tech: I wanted to let you know I'm pregnant.
Pharmacist: Will you be working after the baby is born?
Pharmacy Tech: Oh no, I want to keep this job.

Pharmacy Tech: I think you're overworking the staff.
Pharmacist: Why is that?
Pharmacy Tech: They're wearing toe tags for name badges.

Pharmacy Tech: You're treating me like an old comforter.
Pharmacist: Why do you say that?
Pharmacy Tech: Every time I ask for a raise you turn me down.

Pharmacy Tech: How many people work in your pharmacy?
Pharmacist: About half of them.

Pharmacist: Why are you quitting? Is your pay too low?
Pharmacy Tech: The pay is OK but I feel like I'm keeping a horse out of a job.

Pharmacy Tech: What kind of advice did you give that senior citizen?
Pharmacist: I told him to lessen his tension and enjoy his pension.

Pharmacist: Did she say her husband was in the hospital?
Pharmacy Tech: Yes, she said he was run over by a steam roller and he's in room #312, #313, and #314.

Pharmacy Tech: Can money bring happiness?
Pharmacist: No, but it enables you to look in more places.

Pharmacist: Why didn't you get bucket-seats in your new vehicle?
Pharmacy Tech: Not everyone has the same size bucket.

Pharmacy Tech: Why is experience so important?
Pharmacist: It enables you to recognize a mistake when you make it again.

Pharmacist: Do you have any idea where you are going?
Pharmacy Tech: If you don't know where you're going, you're never lost.

Pharmacist: Why didn't you answer my question?
Pharmacy Tech: A closed mouth gathers no feet.

Pharmacy Tech: Will your conscience keep you from doing wrong?
Pharmacist: No, but it will keep you from enjoying it.

Pharmacy Tech: Why can't you take it with you?
Pharmacist: Because it goes before you do.

Pharmacy Tech: What do you consider middle age?
Pharmacist: When the broadness of your mind and the narrowness of your waist change places.

Pharmacist: What was your problem at the car wash?
Pharmacy Tech: They said my car is so battered and beat up that it scratches their brushes!

Pharmacist: How's your sore throat?
Pharmacy Tech: It feels like the cat has been using it

for a scratching post.

Pharmacist: How's your new diet?
Pharmacy Tech: It's the greatest diet in the world. You can eat whatever you want, whenever you want, and as much as you want. You don't lose any weight but it's easy to stick to.

Pharmacy Tech: What should I give my wife for her birthday. If I give her something practical she'll burst into tears.
Pharmacist: Buy her some handkerchiefs.

Pharmacist: Do you enjoy jogging?
Pharmacy Tech: Yes, but it's that long ride home with the paramedics that gets me.

Pharmacist: Why are you laughing?
Pharmacy Tech: That salesman tried to sell me a laptop computer.
Pharmacist: What's so funny?
Pharmacy Tech: I don't have a lap.

Pharmacist: Why are you mad at the banker?
Pharmacy Tech: They charged me "non-sufficient funds fee" on money they already knew I didn't have.

Pharmacy Tech: What do you mean by "laughing stock?"
Pharmacist: Cattle with a sense of humor.

Pharmacist: Did the mechanic repair your brakes?
Pharmacy Tech: No, but he made my horn louder.

Pharmacist: How can I avoid the 5 o'clock rush?
Pharmacy Tech: Leave at noon.

Pharmacist: Why do you want a drug jacket with short sleeves?
Pharmacy Tech: I'm supporting the right to bare arms.

Pharmacist: What have you learned from jogging?
Pharmacy Tech: I know why race horses never smile.

Pharmacy Tech: Why don't you date women your own age?
Pharmacist: There aren't any.

Pharmacy Tech: How do you know when you're growing old?
Pharmacist: You know you're growing old when tying-one-on means fastening your medic alert bracelet.

Pharmacy Tech: Do you feel like you've grown older?
Pharmacist: Except for an occasional heart attack, I feel as young as I ever did.

Pharmacy Tech: How can I avoid temptation?
Pharmacist: Don't worry about it. As you grow older it will avoid you.

Pharmacy Tech: How will I recognize middle age?
Pharmacist: When you have the choice of two temptations and you choose the one that will get you home earlier, you have reached middle age.

Pharmacy Tech: How would you like your Last Will and Testament to read?
Pharmacist: Being of sound mind, I spent all my money.

Pharmacist: How did you happen to go to Dr. Hermann?
Pharmacy Tech: Well, the gal who works at our cosmetic counter said she has had several of her children by Dr.

Hermann and she said he was really good.

Pharmacist: Are you married?
Pharmacy Tech: No, I'm divorced.
Pharmacist: What did your husband do before you divorced him?
Pharmacy Tech: A lot of things that I didn't know about.

Pharmacist: What is your name?
Pharmacy Tech: My name is Mary Moore.
Pharmacist: What is your marital status?
Pharmacy Tech: Fair.

Pharmacist: Are you qualified to give a urine sample?
Pharmacy Tech: Yes. I have been since early childhood.

Pharmacist: Do you drink when you're on duty?
Pharmacy Tech: Not unless I come to work drunk.

Pharmacy Tech: I asked the doctor how many autopsies he had performed on dead people.
Pharmacist: What did the doctor say?
Pharmacy Tech: He said all of his autopsies have been performed on dead people.

Pharmacists Tech: Did that patient say he was shot in the woods?
Pharmacist: No, he said he was shot in the lumbar region.

Pharmacist: During this interview I would like all your responses to be oral. Are you a certified pharmacy technician?
Pharmacy Tech: Oral.

Pharmacist: Are you a graduate of a recognized pharmacy technician school?
Pharmacy Tech: Oral.

Pharmacy Tech: What does the census taker do?
Pharmacist: He goes from house to house increasing the population.

Pharmacist: Do you know the meaning of H_2O and CO_2?
Pharmacy Tech: H_2O is hot water and CO_2 is cold water.

Pharmacy Tech: What is the salmon run?
Pharmacist: That's when the salmon swim upstream to spoon.

Pharmacy Tech: What is the principle of the X-ray?
Pharmacist: The colder the X-ray table, the more of your body is required on it.

Pharmacy Tech: What do you think of the postal service?
Pharmacist: Bills travel through the mail at twice the speed of checks.

Pharmacist: Don't forget your wife's birthday.
Pharmacy Tech: I'm attempting to get a new car for her. It will be a great trade.

Pharmacy Tech: Why did the pharmacist scale the chain-link fence?
Pharmacist: To see what was on the other side.

Pharmacist: Why do you take your wife everywhere you go?

Pharmacy Tech: I hate to kiss her goodbye.

Pharmacy Tech: How many pharmacists does it take to change a light bulb?
Pharmacist: I'm going to work this one on my calculator, and I think you're going to be pleasantly surprised.

Pharmacist: How many lawyers does it take to change a light bulb?
Pharmacy Tech: Ten, but we'll accept eight.

Pharmacist: How come you were turned down at the blood bank?
Pharmacy Tech: They wanted plasma, not asthma.

Pharmacist: In what state were you born?
Pharmacy Tech: In the nude.

Pharmacy Tech: You say its $2.50 for the cage and $3.00 with the stand?
Pharmacist: Yes, you see, I'm giving you the bird.

Pharmacy Tech: Tomorrow I celebrate my 24th birthday.
Pharmacist: Better late than never.

Pharmacist: How did you break your arm?
Pharmacy Tech: I was trying to pat myself on the back for minding my own business.

Pharmacy Tech: I went to the garage to have the oil changed in my car.
Pharmacist: What did they tell you?
Pharmacy Tech: They told me to keep the oil and change the car.

Pharmacist: When I was born they fired a 21-gun salute.
Pharmacy Tech: Too bad they missed.

Pharmacy Tech: How did the accident happen?
Pharmacist: My wife fell asleep in the back seat of the car.

Pharmacy Tech: I suppose all you male pharmacists like wine, women, and song?
Pharmacist: We don't care much for music.

Pharmacy Tech: That soldier at the prescription counter said he is a West Pointer.
Pharmacist: He looks like an Irish Setter to me.

Pharmacist: When I was seven years old my father took me to the zoo.
Pharmacy Tech: Were you accepted?

Pharmacist: What time do you start work?
Pharmacy Tech: About two hours after I get here.

Pharmacist: I wish you wouldn't whistle while you work.
Pharmacy Tech: Who's working?

Pharmacist: Why do you think your wife is getting tired of you?
Pharmacy Tech: She keeps wrapping my lunch in road maps.

Pharmacy Tech: How can you make money selling watches so cheap?
Pharmacist: Easy, we make a profit repairing them.

Pharmacist: I don't look 35, do I?
Pharmacy Tech: No, but I'll bet you did when you were.

Pharmacy Tech: My doctor told me I needed a change of climate.
Pharmacist: You're in luck, according to the weather report, it's coming tomorrow.

Pharmacist: How did you find the weather when you were in Arizona?
Pharmacy Tech: I just went outside and there it was.

Pharmacist: What is that fly doing in my cup of coffee?
Pharmacy Tech: It looks like the back stroke to me.

Pharmacy Tech: Why were you flirting with the waitress?
Pharmacist: I was playing for bigger steaks.

Pharmacy Tech: How can I get my husband to do sit-ups?
Pharmacist: Put the remote control at his feet.

Pharmacy Tech: What is the reason most people take aspirin?
Pharmacist: For a headache.
Pharmacy Tech: Who wants a headache?

Pharmacy Tech: What is the greatest miracle of modern medicine?
Pharmacist: The person who discovered how to get 50,000 units of vitamin D in a single capsule.
Pharmacy Tech: Who was he?
Pharmacist: A school bus driver.

Pharmacy Tech: He wants to buy some rat poison.
Pharmacist: Should I wrap it or does he want to take it here?

Pharmacy Tech: I told him that you said he should stop taking those pills as they could become habit forming.
Pharmacist: What did he say?
Pharmacy Tech: He said you didn't know what you are talking about. He's been taking them for 12 years.

Pharmacy Tech: What is your new mother-in-law sandwich?
Pharmacist: Cold shoulder and salty tongue.

Pharmacy Tech: Why can't you fire that bookkeeper?
Pharmacist: She's the only one who understands the filing system.

Pharmacy Tech: Why did you decide not to put in the bakery?
Pharmacist: I couldn't raise the dough.

Pharmacy Tech: How can you tell which one is the boss?
Pharmacist: He's the one who watches the clock during the coffee break.

Pharmacist: What does she mean they are having a picnic?
Pharmacy Tech: She means the boss is on vacation.

Pharmacy Tech: What is the most dangerous position to sleep in?
Pharmacist: With your feet on the desk at work.

Pharmacist: Why do you go for a haircut on company time?
Pharmacy Tech: Because it grew on company time.

Pharmacy Tech: How has business been?
Pharmacist: It's usually very slow in the morning but it drops off after lunch.

Pharmacy Tech: He wants to know who will know what to do until the doctor answers?
Pharmacist: Tell him to talk to the doctor's wife.

Pharmacy Tech: What is the chief mission of the medical profession?
Pharmacist: When the patient is at death's door, it is the duty of the physician to pull him through.

Pharmacy Tech: What do you mean by a naturopathic physician?
Pharmacist: Nature cures but the physician sends the bill.

Pharmacy Tech: Why do you sometimes say physician instead of doctor?
Pharmacist: A man who is sick calls a doctor; a man

who becomes ill calls a physician.

Pharmacist: Can you tell me the structural formula, mode of action, side effects and dosage range for hexamethylenetet-ramine.
Pharmacy Tech: No.

Pharmacist: Have you had any surgical operations?
Pharmacy Tech: Yes, when I was four days old.

Pharmacist: I must be getting older.
Pharmacy Tech: Why is that?
Pharmacist: My wife said I could hire our new bookkeeper.

Pharmacy Tech: What did you tell your young son?
Pharmacist: I told him that if he didn't eat his lunch, he wouldn't grow up to be big and strong and be a pharmacist, like his daddy, and not have time to eat his lunch.

Pharmacy Tech: He gets his prescription filled religiously.
Pharmacist: What do you mean, religiously?
Pharmacy Tech: He swears every time he pays for it.

Pharmacist: What seems to be your husband's problem?
Pharmacy Tech: He has flat feet.
Pharmacist: Maybe he can't help it.
Pharmacy Tech: He can, he always has his feet in the wrong flat.

Pharmacy Tech: I didn't keep my appointment with that doctor you recommended.
Pharmacist: Why didn't you see him?
Pharmacy Tech: The sign on his door said 9 to 1. I want better odds than that.

Pharmacy Tech: He said he has a case of beriberi. What shall I tell him?
Pharmacist: Tell him to wait until we lock up and we'll help him drink it.

Pharmacy Tech: Who are the best doctors you ever heard of?
Pharmacist: Dr. Diet, Dr. Quiet, and Dr. Merryman.

Pharmacy Tech: I told him you couldn't tell him the cause of his problem but it's probably due to drinking.
Pharmacist: What did he say?
Pharmacy Tech: He said he'd come back when you're sober.

Pharmacist: Are you familiar with Gray's Anatomy?
Pharmacy Tech: Sir, I am familiar with no man's anatomy!

Pharmacy Tech: We should teach that new college girl clerk what is right and what is wrong.
Pharmacist: Good idea. You teach her what's right.

Pharmacist: A little knowledge is dangerous.
Pharmacy Tech: Then, how come what you don't know won't hurt you?

Pharmacist: What do you know about Red China?
Pharmacy Tech: It looks good on a white table cloth.

Pharmacy Tech: I'd like to marry your daughter.
Pharmacist: Have you seen her mother?
Pharmacy Tech: Yes, but I'd prefer to marry your daughter.

Pharmacist: I see from your application that you have been fired from your last four jobs.

Pharmacy Tech: Yes, and that's positive proof that I am not a quitter.

Pharmacist: Thank you. I've never enjoyed a dance so much.
Pharmacy Tech: Oh! Then you have danced before?

Pharmacy Tech: Every pharmacist should have at least one pharmacy tech.
Pharmacist: Why is that?
Pharmacy Tech: Sooner or later something will go wrong and he will need someone to blame it on.

Pharmacy Tech: As I've been telling you ever since I started, you don't know how to run a pharmacy.
Pharmacist: I like a girl who has the courage to stand up to her boss and tell him just what she thinks of him. You're fired!

Pharmacy Tech: The doctor advised my husband to give up golf.
Pharmacist: Is it his feet?
Pharmacy Tech: No, the doctor saw him playing.

Pharmacist to Pharmacy Tech: My wife and I have been married for 40 years. There is nothing in this world I wouldn't do for her, and there is nothing in this world she wouldn't do for me. That's why in the last 40 years neither of us has done a thing for the other.

Pharmacy Tech: I'm a father! Have a cigar.
Pharmacist: Thanks. Is it a boy or a girl?
Pharmacy Tech: I don't know. All cigars look alike to me.

Pharmacy Tech: Your coffee cup is empty, would you like another ?
Pharmacist: Why would I want two empty coffee cups?

Pharmacist: I am looking for someone who is honest, reliable and not afraid of hard work.
Pharmacy Tech: Hire me and I'll help you look.

Pharmacist: They say the lie detector is quite an instrument. Have you ever seen one?
Pharmacy Tech: Seen one? I married one!

Pharmacist: I have tickets to the theater, would you like to go.
Pharmacy Tech: I'd love to. I'll go home and get ready.
Pharmacist: That's a good idea, go ahead. The tickets are for tomorrow night.

Pharmacy Tech: You say you are divorcing your husband because he's careless about his appearance?
Pharmacist: That's right. He hasn't shown up for three months.

Pharmacy Tech: I read that matrimonial column in the newspaper about that lonely widow who was looking for a husband. I wrote her a letter and sent a photograph.
Pharmacist: What did she say?
Pharmacy Tech: She said she wasn't that lonely.

Pharmacist: Why do you always use the drive-up window at the bank?
Pharmacy Tech: I think it's only right that I let my car see its real owner now and then.

Pharmacist: When I was your age I used to use face cream every night.
Pharmacy Tech: Yes, and look at your face now.

Pharmacist: I think the best thing for you to do is give up smoking and drinking.
Pharmacy Tech: I don't deserve the best; what's the second best?

Pharmacist's daughter: Daddy, I've finally found the man I love.
Pharmacist: Does he have any money?
Pharmacists daughter: You men are all alike. That's the first question he asked me about you.

Pharmacy Tech: I'm reading a book about three Spaniards who traveled 3,000 miles on a galleon!
Pharmacist: You can't believe everything you read about those small foreign cars.

Pharmacy Tech: I would like to have tomorrow off.
Pharmacist: Why do you want tomorrow off?
Pharmacy Tech: It's our 25th wedding anniversary and we'd like to celebrate.
Pharmacist: Do you mean to tell me your going to expect to do this every 25 years?

Pharmacy Tech: You're wearing your wedding ring on the wrong finger.
Pharmacist: I married the wrong woman.

Pharmacist: Who was driving at the time of the accident?
Pharmacy Tech: My wife was.
Pharmacist: Where were you sitting?

Humor in Pharmacy

Pharmacy Tech: I was behind the steering wheel.

Pharmacist: Have you finished the book I lent you last week?
Pharmacy Tech: I'm really sorry but I lent it to a friend. Did you want it back?
Pharmacist: Not for myself, but the fellow I borrowed it from said the owner was looking for it.

Pharmacy Tech: Bingo has given me the happiest days of my life.
Pharmacist: I thought you said you never play Bingo.
Pharmacy Tech: I don't, my wife does.

Pharmacy Tech: How did you wish your wife a Happy Birthday?
Pharmacist: I said it with flowers. I sent her a rose.
Pharmacy Tech: Only one rose?
Pharmacist: I'm a man of few words.

Pharmacist: You phoned in sick last Friday and said you couldn't work but I understand you were at the football game.
Pharmacy Tech: That wasn't me at the football game, it was another fellow who looks like me.
Pharmacist: How do you know that?
Pharmacy Tech: I was there and I saw him.

Pharmacist: My wife said she wanted something with diamonds on it for her birthday.
Pharmacy Tech: What did you give her?
Pharmacist: A deck of playing cards.

Pharmacy Tech: How can you spot a psychiatrist in a nudist camp?

Pharmacist: He's the one who's listening and not looking.

Pharmacist: What do you call a geriatric gynecologist?
Pharmacy Tech: I don't know, what do you call one?
Pharmacist: He's a spreader of old wives tails.

Pharmacy Tech: What's new in product development?
Pharmacist: A new tablet that is half aspirin and half glue. It's for splitting headaches.

Pharmacist: What ever happened to that steady, old carry-out customer?
Pharmacy Tech: He starved to death trying to unwrap his last sandwich.

Pharmacist: Why didn't you pay the psychiatrist for curing you of gambling?
Pharmacy Tech: We tossed double or nothing and I won.

Pharmacy Tech: I asked him if he was taking his medicine regularly.
Pharmacist: What did he say?
Pharmacy Tech: He said that when he received our bill he decided to keep on coughing.

Pharmacy Tech: Your wife wants you to call her at home.
Pharmacist: Tell her I don't make home calls.

Pharmacist: Ask him if the nurse took his pulse.
Pharmacy Tech: He said she didn't take it, he still has it.

Pharmacy Tech: He said he never felt so bad in his life.
Pharmacist: Tell him to go see Dr. Silverman, he'll never live to regret it.

Pharmacy Tech: He said there is something wrong with his stomach.
Pharmacist: Tell him to keep his coat buttoned and nobody will notice it.

Pharmacist: You should think about becoming a doctor.
Pharmacy Tech: Why do you say that?
Pharmacist: Because you have the handwriting for it.

Pharmacist: Why is she so unhappy with the doctor?
Pharmacy Tech: She said her child swallowed a nickel and the doctor made her cough up $10.

Pharmacy Tech: Will an apple a day keep the doctor away?
Pharmacist: Yes, and an onion a day will keep everyone away.

Pharmacist: Was the doctor able to help her?
Pharmacy Tech: No. She said he felt her purse and said there was nothing he could do.

Pharmacist: Did he say why he couldn't pay his bill?
Pharmacy Tech: He said he slowed down like the doctor told him to do and he lost his job.

Pharmacy Tech: What do you mean when you say the doctor has it made?
Pharmacist: He's the only man who can tell a woman to take off her clothes and then send her husband a bill for it.

Pharmacy Tech: Would you like to see where I was operated on for appendicitis?
Pharmacist: No, I hate to look at hospitals.

Pharmacist: How long have you been out of work?
Pharmacy Tech: I don't know, I lost my birth certificate.

Pharmacist: Did she say why her husband is in the hospital?
Pharmacy Tech: She said it was his knee. She found a strange woman on it.

Pharmacist: How is his office nurse?
Pharmacy Tech: She couldn't put a dressing on a salad.

Pharmacist: Were you worried?
Pharmacy Tech: I was on pills and needles all week.

Pharmacist: Why are you asking for a raise?
Pharmacy Tech: Well, actually, somehow my family found out that other people eat three times a day.

Pharmacist: Why did you complain about the nurse?
Pharmacy Tech: Because she kept giving me nuts when I asked for dates.

Pharmacy Tech: Do I have to do that?
Pharmacist: Only if you want to keep your job.

Pharmacist: What do you mean you're not late?
Pharmacy Tech: Because I took my coffee break before I came in.

Pharmacy Tech: Why is he saving old magazines?
Pharmacist: He's studying to be a dentist.

Pharmacy Tech: What kind of a husband do you think I should look for?

Pharmacist: I think you better leave the husbands alone and look for a single man.

Pharmacist: Is your husband hard to please?
Pharmacy Tech: I don't know, I've never tried.

Pharmacist: Why do you think your husband is tired of you?
Pharmacy Tech: He hasn't been home for four years.

Pharmacist: Would you mind getting my broker on the phone?
Pharmacy Tech: Stock or pawn?

Pharmacist: How many words can you type a minute?
Pharmacy Tech: Big ones or little ones?

Pharmacy Tech: Who introduced you to your wife?
Pharmacist: We just met. I can't blame anyone.

Pharmacy Tech: If you were my husband, I'd give you poison.
Pharmacist: If you were my wife, I'd take it.

Pharmacy Tech: What do you think about people who go to a psychiatrist?
Pharmacist: They need to have their head examined.

Pharmacist: I understand you've been coming to work late.
Pharmacy Tech: Yes, but I go home early.

Pharmacist: Why do you sleep in a bathing suit?
Pharmacy Tech: Because my hot water bottle leaks.

Pharmacy Tech: What should I take for my cold?
Pharmacist: Don't refuse any offer.

Pharmacy Tech: I have my husband eating out of my hand.
Pharmacist: Saves lots of dishes, doesn't it?

Pharmacist: What do you mean your wife is a careful driver?
Pharmacy Tech: She always slows down for a red light.

Pharmacist: I don't intend to be married until I'm 30.
Pharmacy Tech: I don't intend to be 30 until I'm married.

Pharmacist: I hear Brady is getting married.
Pharmacy Tech: Serves him right, I never did like that guy.

Pharmacist: Why wouldn't the nurse give you a bedpan?
Pharmacy Tech: She said she was a head nurse.

Pharmacist: Never hit a man when he's down.
Pharmacy Tech: Why not?
Pharmacist: He might get up again.

Pharmacy Tech: Why do you say that men make the best salesmen.
Pharmacist: Because they're used to taking orders.

Pharmacist: Why do you keep your money in the refrigerator?
Pharmacy Tech: Because I like to have cold cash.

Pharmacy Tech: Where would I be if I had a million dollars?
Pharmacist: You'd be on our honeymoon.

Pharmacist: You say your mother-in-law visited you only once?
Pharmacy Tech: Yes, she came the day we were married and she never left.

Pharmacist: How is your typing?
Pharmacy Tech: Not so bad if you compare it with my handwriting.

Pharmacy Tech: What is a practical nurse?
Pharmacist: A nurse who marries a rich patient.

Pharmacy Tech: Why do doctors wear those masks when they're in the operating room?
Pharmacist: That's so that if something goes wrong nobody can identify them.

Pharmacy Tech: The doctor said I have insomnia.
Pharmacist: Don't lose any sleep over it.

Pharmacy Tech: Every day when I come home from work my wife never cooks, she throws dishes at me and she calls me awful names. What do you think is wrong?
Pharmacist: Off hand, I would say she doesn't like you.

Pharmacist: How does your psychiatrist cure your alcoholism?
Pharmacy Tech: He charges so much you can't afford liquor.

Pharmacist: What did Whistler say when he saw his mother standing by the window?
Pharmacy Tech: He said, "Mother, you're off your rocker!"

Pharmacist: Were you ever troubled with pneumonia.

Pharmacy Tech: Only when I tried to spell it.

Pharmacist: Why has your illness lasted so long?
Pharmacy Tech: I'm too weak to get well and too strong to get sick.

Pharmacy Tech: On our farm we go to bed with the chickens.
Pharmacist: At our house we prefer to sleep in a bed.

Pharmacy Tech: What is the best way for a girl to keep her youth?
Pharmacist: Don't introduce him to anyone.

Pharmacist: What happened to your garage?
Pharmacy Tech: My wife backed the car out of the garage but she forgot that she backed it in the night before.

Pharmacist: When you got married, why did you go to the altar with your hair in rollers?
Pharmacy Tech: Because I wanted to look good at the reception.

Pharmacy Tech: How do you know that autumn is here?
Pharmacist: I just got my air conditioner back from repair.

Pharmacist: Are you having any trouble meeting expenses?
Pharmacy Tech: No, my wife keeps introducing me to new ones.

Pharmacist: What did the sign in the singles bar say?
Pharmacy Tech: The sign said: MEN: NO SHIRTS, NO SERVE. WOMEN: NO SHIRT, NO CHECK.

Humor in Pharmacy

Pharmacist: Who told you that you could loaf around the drug store just because I kissed you last week?
Pharmacy Tech: My lawyer.

Pharmacist: I understand your wife delivered triplets. The Lord has smiled at you.
Pharmacy Tech: Smiled at me, he laughed out loud.

Pharmacy Tech: That patient told me the doctor said he would give him three months to live and he told the doctor it would take him six months to pay off his bill.
Pharmacist: What did the doctor say to that?
Pharmacy Tech: The doctor said in that case he would give him six months to live.

Pharmacist: How's your sore back coming along?
Pharmacy Tech: If it doesn't get better in a week, I'm going to the emergency room.

Pharmacist: Do you like working for this company?
Pharmacy Tech: I'd work for this company for nothing if the price was right.

Pharmacy Tech: Is it OK to destroy those old prescription files?
Pharmacist: Yes, but be sure to make copies of them first.

Pharmacy Tech: He said his wife is at death's door.
Pharmacist: Tell him this prescription will pull her through.

Pharmacy Tech: He wants to know if we have any licorice root.
Pharmacist: Tell him if it's in stock, we got it.

Pharmacist: Why do you need the day off?
Pharmacy Tech: If you don't go to other people's funerals, they don't come to yours.

Pharmacist: Can I depend on you to be honest with me?
Pharmacy Tech: Yes. I won't tell you any half truths unless they're completely honest.

Pharmacist: Why do you want to live to be 100?
Pharmacy Tech: Because few people die past the age of 100.

Pharmacy Tech: How is the new janitor working out?
Pharmacist: We're overpaying him, but he's worth it.

Pharmacy Tech: He said the doctor told him he had chronic constipation.
Pharmacist: Tell him anything that doctor tells him should be taken with a dose of salts.

Pharmacy Tech: He said he tried diuretic tablets 10 years ago.
Pharmacist: Tell him we've all passed a lot of water since then.

Pharmacist: Things are moving too fast.
Pharmacy Tech: There's no stopping the future.

Pharmacist: What were you and that customer talking about?
Pharmacy Tech: I've got the same condition he has, only mine is much worse.

Pharmacy Tech: What shall I tell the patient?

Pharmacist: It's most important to tell the truth, even if you have to lie to do so.

Pharmacy Tech: Did your wife like her surprise birthday gift?
Pharmacist: She always loves a surprise gift, especially if it's something she picked out.

Pharmacy Tech: Have you ever been wrong?
Pharmacist: Only once. I thought I was wrong but I wasn't.

Pharmacist: Have you looked at the new edition of the United States Pharmacopoeia?
Pharmacy Tech: I've read parts of it all the way through.

Pharmacy Tech: We're going to call our new son Michael.
Pharmacist: Every Tom, Dick, and Harry is called Michael.

Pharmacy Tech: Would you like to know what I think?
Pharmacist: When I want your opinion, I'll give it to you.

Pharmacist: Why don't you go to Herby's Diner for lunch anymore?
Pharmacy Tech: Nobody goes there anymore, it's too crowded.

Pharmacy Tech: Do you want me to give you an honest answer?
Pharmacist: Don't let your opinions sway your judgment.

Pharmacy Tech: How do you think she looks?
Pharmacist: If she wasn't so skinny, I'd consider her to be thin.

Pharmacist: Why did you buy two neckties?
Pharmacy Tech: I got one in navy blue and I also liked the
one in navy brown.

Pharmacist: What time is it?
Pharmacy Tech: Do you mean right now?

Pharmacy Tech: Are you sure you're right about that?
Pharmacist: I might not always be right, but I'm never
wrong.

Pharmacy Tech: How can I help to make the company
newsletter a success?
Pharmacist: Make sure that all the i's are crossed and
all the t's are dotted.

Pharmacist: What did you accomplish today?
Pharmacy Tech: I did nothing all day and I still didn't get it
done.

Pharmacist: What's your favorite sport?
Pharmacy Tech: Football. I love football and I watch a lot of
it on radio.

Pharmacist: Is there a lot of crime in your neighborhood?
Pharmacy Tech: A lot of crime? I wouldn't go out at night
alone unless someone was with me.

Pharmacy Tech: What did you tell him when he said he
thought health care is expensive?
Pharmacist: I told him if he thinks it's expensive now, wait
until he sees how expensive it is when it's free.

Pharmacist: What did he say about his x-rays?
Pharmacy Tech: He said the doctor x-rayed his head and found nothing.

Pharmacist: Have you ever considered a blind date?
Pharmacy Tech: I'd rather go out with a perfect stranger than go out on a blind date.

Pharmacist: What do you think about the new nudist colony?
Pharmacy Tech: If God had meant for people to go nude they would have been born that way.

Pharmacist: How did you get to know her?
Pharmacy Tech: We went to different schools together.

Pharmacist: What did she say about her husband?
Pharmacy Tech: She said he is home from the hospital but he's still in bed at night with a special nurse.

Pharmacist: What did she say her husband died of?
Pharmacy Tech: She said he tested every single cure given in his home medical book and he died of a typographical error.

Pharmacy Tech: What is the most important qualification to get a job here?
Pharmacist: A small appetite.

Pharmacist: What does the sign at the luncheonette say?
Pharmacy Tech: It says, "FRIENDLY, COURTEOUS, EFFICIENT, PROMPT SELF-SERVICE."

Pharmacist: What did that senior citizen say about retirement?
Pharmacy Tech: He said retirement is a time when you can

do absolutely, positively, anything you want to do . . . providing it's free!

Pharmacist: Why did he say he took up jogging?
Pharmacy Tech: He said it was the only way he could hear heavy breathing again.

Pharmacist: My son couldn't decide between a two-year and a four-year college.
Pharmacy Tech: What did he decide to go?
Pharmacist: He compromised. He went to a two-year college for four years.

Pharmacy Tech: It's the squeaking wheel that gets the grease.
Pharmacist: Not always. Sometimes it gets replaced.

Pharmacy Tech: If I catch a cold should I call in a good doctor?
Pharmacist: No, call in three good doctors and play bridge.

Pharmacist: What did he say about the divorce?
Pharmacy Tech: He said his wife thought he was worthless but her lawyer thought differently.

Pharmacy Tech: He wants to know if we have anything for gray hair.
Pharmacist: Tell him we have nothing but respect.

Pharmacist: What did he say about success?
Pharmacy Tech: He said he can remember when people dressed for success, not undressed.

Pharmacist: Do you miss being a teenager?
Pharmacy Tech: No, but I'm still looking for a place to park

but for a different reason.

Pharmacy Tech: What's your formula for family success?
Pharmacist: The family that invests in CDs together stays together.

Pharmacist: What are your three strongest motivations to come to work each morning?
Pharmacy Tech: Visa, Master Charge, and American Express.

Pharmacy Tech: Why do you say laughter is the best medicine?
Pharmacist: Because it needs no prescription, has no unpleasant taste, and it costs nothing.

Pharmacy Tech: What is Nitrate of Sodium?
Pharmacist: Half the day rate, I suppose.

Pharmacy Tech: Why do you envy a bachelor?
Pharmacist: He's entitled to life, liberty, and the happiness of pursuit.

Pharmacy Tech: What would you administer to a person who has just swallowed 50 phenobarbital tablets?
Pharmacist: The last sacraments.

Pharmacy Tech: Why do you think God gave women a sense of humor?
Pharmacist: So they could understand the jokes they married.

Pharmacy Tech: Why do you say that laughter is like changing a baby's diaper?
Pharmacist: It doesn't solve any problems permanently, it

just makes life a bit more comfortable for a while.

Pharmacist: Ask him if the doctor treated him yesterday.
Pharmacy Tech: He said no, he charged him $10.

Pharmacist: Why did you get divorced?
Pharmacy Tech: We talked about taking a vacation or getting a divorce. We decided that a trip to Hawaii would be over in a week but a divorce is something we would have forever.

Pharmacy Tech: What is the difference between an optimist and a pessimist?
Pharmacist: An optimist laughs to forget. A pessimist forgets to laugh.

Pharmacy Tech: He said he's going to have brain surgery.
Pharmacist: He needs brain surgery like he needs a hole in his head.

Pharmacy Tech: What's the difference between an itch and an allergy?
Pharmacist: About $30 an appointment.

Pharmacy Tech: My doctor made appointments for me to see two other doctors.
Pharmacist: Is he a doctor or a booking agent?

Pharmacy Tech: What are the first two things a doctor learns in medical school?
Pharmacist: The first two things thing they learn are to scribble their prescriptions so no one can read them and to type out their bills so everyone can read them.

Pharmacy Tech: He said the doctor wanted to give his wife

a local anesthetic.
Pharmacist: What did he tell the doctor?
Pharmacy Tech: He told the doctor that he could afford the best. Give her something imported.

Pharmacy Tech: He told the doctor he didn't feel so good.
Pharmacist: What did the doctor say?
Pharmacy Tech: He said, "Let me give you a complete checkup. You'll never live to regret it."

Pharmacy Tech: I heard they took away that doctor's license because he was having an affair with one of his patients.
Pharmacist: That's right and it's really too bad. He was one of our best veterinarians.

Pharmacy Tech: Does that doctor make house calls?
Pharmacist: No, but if you are sick more than five days he sends you a get-well card.

Pharmacy Tech: He said he asked the doctor what is the best thing to take when you're run down.
Pharmacist: What did the doctor tell him?
Pharmacy Tech: The doctor told him to take down the license plate number.

Pharmacist: Did he say his hospital stay was successful?
Pharmacy Tech: He said he's OK but his savings died.

Pharmacy Tech: Why do you say doctors and lawyers are a lot alike?
Pharmacist: Because, win, lose, or draw, they get paid.

Pharmacy Tech: He told the doctor he had a terrible pain in his back every time he bends over.

Pharmacist: What did the doctor tell him?
Pharmacy Tech: The doctor told him not to bend over.

Pharmacy Tech: When will the doctor give him the shock treatment?
Pharmacist: When he sends him the bill.

Pharmacy Tech: He said the doctor put him on his feet in no time at all.
Pharmacist: How did the doctor do that?
Pharmacy Tech: He made him sell his car to pay the bill.

Pharmacy Tech: He said he asked the doctor, "How do I stand?"
Pharmacist: What did the doctor say?
Pharmacy Tech: The doctor said, "I don't know. It's a miracle."

Pharmacy Tech: He said the doctor gave him good news and bad news.
Pharmacist: What was it?
Pharmacy Tech: The bad news was they amputated the wrong foot. The good news was, the fellow in the other bed wanted to buy his shoes.

Pharmacy Tech: He said his wife presented him with a pair of loafers for his birthday.
Pharmacist: Does he mean bedroom slippers?
Pharmacy Tech: No, he means her two brothers.

Pharmacist: Why did she stop taking tranquilizers?
Pharmacy Tech: Because she found herself being pleasant to people she didn't care for.

Pharmacy Tech: He said he dreamed all night that he was eating shredded wheat.
Pharmacist: What happened when he woke up?
Pharmacy Tech: Half the mattress was gone.

Pharmacy Tech: What advice did you give him when he said he was being admitted to the hospital?
Pharmacist: I said if he tries to kiss the nurse, he should be sure to remove the thermometer from his mouth first.

Pharmacy Tech: He said all last week he ate nothing but hundred dollar-a-plate dinners.
Pharmacist: What restaurant was he in?
Pharmacy Tech: He wasn't in a restaurant, he was in the hospital.

Pharmacist: What makes him think his surgery was so serious?
Pharmacy Tech: As soon as they finished the surgery they put him in the expensive care unit.

Pharmacist: Did her doctor treat her with acupuncture?
Pharmacy Tech: No, the only thing he stuck her with was his bill.

Pharmacist: What do you mean, they divorced because of illness?
Pharmacy Tech: They got sick of each other.

Pharmacist: Why do you say you and your wife were incompatible?
Pharmacy Tech: My wife hated me when I was drunk and I couldn't stand her when I was sober.

Pharmacist: What did the doctor tell him?

Pharmacy Tech: He said the softness of his muscles is exceeded only by the hardness of his arteries.

Pharmacy Tech: He asked if this medicine has side effects.
Pharmacist: Tell him just one, poverty.

Pharmacy Tech: He was telling me how they gave him a bath in the hospital.
Pharmacist: How did they do it?
Pharmacy Tech: He said the nurse washed down as far as possible and then she washed up as far as possible. Then she handed him a wet cloth and stepped out of the room while he washed possible.

Pharmacy Tech: He said he asked the doctor if he made house calls.
Pharmacist: What did the doctor tell him?
Pharmacy Tech: He said the only people who make house calls anymore are plumbers, TV repairmen, and burglars.

Pharmacy Tech: He said the doctor told him he couldn't make him young again.
Pharmacist: What did he tell the doctor?
Pharmacy Tech: He told him he didn't want to get younger, he just wanted to get older.

Pharmacy Tech: The doctor told him he had just three days to live, who would he like to see?
Pharmacist: What did he tell the doctor?
Pharmacy Tech: He told him he wanted to see another doctor.

Pharmacist: How did the doctor tell her to take care of her new baby?
Pharmacy Tech: She said he told her to keep one end full

and the other end dry.

Pharmacy Tech: The doctor told him he is in great shape for a man of 75.
Pharmacist: What's wrong with that?
Pharmacy Tech: He's only 36.

Pharmacy Tech: How did the doctor cure her of being a hypochondriac?
Pharmacist: He told her that her insurance didn't cover it.

Pharmacy Tech: Why does she think he's the meanest doctor in town?
Pharmacist: She said he keeps his stethoscope in the freezer.

Pharmacist: Why is he mad at the doctor?
Pharmacy Tech: The doctor told him to stop smoking. Then, he offered him five dollars for his lighter.

Pharmacy Tech: Why did they divorce for religious reasons?
Pharmacist: She worshiped money and he didn't have any.

Pharmacy Tech: What kind of an accident did the tree surgeon have?
Pharmacist: I understand he fell out of his patient.

Pharmacist: What did he say happened when he called the acupuncturist in the middle of the night about his back pain?
Pharmacy Tech: He said the acupuncturist told him to take two thumb tacks and call him in the morning.

Pharmacy Tech: Why was the doctors strike unsuccessful?

Pharmacist: Nobody could read their picket signs.

Pharmacist: Is she happy with the medicare program?
Pharmacy Tech: Yes, she said she's now able to have diseases that used to be beyond her means.

Pharmacy Tech: What is your definition of a doctor?
Pharmacist: A doctor is a person who acts like a humanitarian and charges like a plumber.

Pharmacist: Why did he say he thinks surgeons are getting younger all the time?
Pharmacy Tech: He said one came into his room with his rubber gloves pinned to his shirt cuffs.

Pharmacy Tech: She said she thanked the doctor for the wonderful care he had given her and asked him how she could ever repay him?
Pharmacist: What did the doctor tell her?
Pharmacy Tech: He said, "By cash, check, credit card, or money order.

Pharmacist: Are you a clock watcher?
Pharmacy Tech: No, I'm a bell listener.

Pharmacy Tech: Why do you think there are so many divorces?
Pharmacist: Because too many girls are getting married before they can support a husband.

Pharmacy Tech: He said he was in the hospital for 10 days and got a card that said, "Get well quick."
Pharmacist: Who was it from?
Pharmacy Tech: Blue Cross.

Pharmacy Tech: He said he lit his cigar with a $20 bill.
Pharmacist: He must be extravagant.
Pharmacy Tech: No, it was the doctor's bill.

Pharmacy Tech: My wife wants some pearls for her birthday.
Pharmacist: Give her an oyster and a rabbit's foot.

Pharmacy Tech: That new waitress was waiting on the doctor and scratching herself. The doctor asked her if she had hemorrhoids.
Pharmacist: What did she say?
Pharmacy Tech: She said, "Sorry, just what's on the menu — no special orders."

Pharmacy Tech: Do old accountants ever die?
Pharmacist: No, they just lose their balance.

Pharmacy Tech: He said he paid the psychiatrist $50 to cure his inferiority complex.
Pharmacist: Did it work?
Pharmacy Tech: Yes, but he got fined $100 for talking back to a highway patrolman.

Pharmacy Tech: That senior citizen said she and her sister went for a tramp in the woods.
Pharmacist: What happened?
Pharmacy Tech: He got away.

Pharmacist: What's his problem?
Pharmacy Tech: He said he has horrible nightmares. One night he dreams he's an Indian teepee. The next night he dreams he's a wigwam.
Pharmacist: He's too tents.

Pharmacy Tech: He said he never misses a sports event so they asked him to speak at the athletic banquet.
Pharmacist: I know, I was there. They introduced him as an old athletic supporter.

Pharmacy Tech: What's your philosophy on marriage.
Pharmacist: Basically it's an institution that separates the men from the joys.

Pharmacy Tech: This suit I'm wearing was made in London.
Pharmacist: It looks like you swam back in it.

Pharmacy Tech: He wants to know if we have Prince Albert in the can?
Pharmacist: Tell him Prince Albert has been in the can for 70 years.

Pharmacist: What did the doctor tell him?
Pharmacy Tech: The doctor said he has the body of a 20-year-old — a 20-year-old Chevrolet.

Pharmacy Tech: When the doctor told him what was wrong with him, he asked for a second opinion.
Pharmacist: What did the doctor say?
Pharmacy Tech: The doctor said, "OK, you're ugly, too.

Pharmacy Tech: He said the doctor told him he had two weeks to live.
Pharmacist: What did he tell the doctor?
Pharmacy Tech: He said, I hope they're not in August!"

Pharmacy Tech: He said he told the doctor he looked in the mirror and he thought he was looking at a dead man. He said he has no color to his skin, his cheeks are sunken in,

and his hair is falling out. What is the problem?
Pharmacist: What did the doctor say?
Pharmacy Tech: The doctor said he didn't know but he was
sure of one thing — his eye sight is great.

Pharmacist: What did the doctor tell him when he gave
him this prescription?
Pharmacy Tech: The doctor said to let him know if the
medicine works, he has the same thing himself.

Pharmacy Tech: What do you mean they are incompatible?
Pharmacist: He's on Valium and she's on Xanax.

Pharmacy Tech: Were there drug problems when you were a
boy?
Pharmacist: There was only one — where to get a
prescription filled on Sunday.

Pharmacy Tech: Will this prescription relax him?
Pharmacist: No, but it will make him enjoy feeling tense.

Pharmacy Tech: Did you say he is a psychiatrist and a
specialist in proctology?
Pharmacist: That's right. He's can treat both odds and
ends.

Pharmacy Tech: Can money buy happiness?
Pharmacist: No, but it can make misery a lot more fun.

Pharmacist: What did the sign in the reducing salon say?
Pharmacy Tech: It said: REAR TODAY—GONE
TOMORROW.

Pharmacy Tech: Is your wife an active Catholic?

Pharmacist: We have so many candles in our house we can't buy fire insurance.

Pharmacy Tech: He said the surgeon told him that having a vasectomy was a very serious matter. He told him to discuss it with his wife first.
Pharmacist: What did she say?
Pharmacy Tech: She said to ask the kids and they voted for it 12 to six.

Pharmacist: How did his appointment with the new doctor go?
Pharmacy Tech: He said the doctor found out what he had — and took it.

Pharmacist: Did he say if the new doctor is expensive?
Pharmacy Tech: He said the doctor charges $40 dollars for a house call — and more if he has to dial the number himself.

Pharmacy Tech: Did the doctor tell you what this patient's problem is?
Pharmacist: The doctor told me the patient said he was a kleptomaniac and wanted to know if there was something he could take for it.

Pharmacy Tech: He said he told the doctor he was having a difficult time breathing.
Pharmacist: What did the doctor say?
Pharmacy Tech: He said the doctor said he would give him something that would stop that.

Pharmacy Tech: What ever happened to that lonely proctologist?
Pharmacist: He looked up a few of his friends.

Pharmacy Tech: He said the doctor told him to give up half of his sex life.
Pharmacist: What did he tell the doctor?
Pharmacy Tech: He asked the doctor which half he should give up, talking about it or thinking about it.

Pharmacy Tech: I asked her if she had recovered from her operation.
Pharmacist: What did she say?
Pharmacy Tech: She said, no, she still has three more payments.

Pharmacy Tech: She said she told the doctor that this morning when she went to the bathroom she passed five pennies. Then, this afternoon she went again and this time she passed dimes and quarters.
Pharmacist: What did the doctor tell her?
Pharmacy Tech: The doctor said she was just going through her change.

Pharmacist: Why do you say you came from a small town?
Pharmacy Tech: The dentist's office was the public library.

Pharmacy Tech: Why did the doctor close his practice?
Pharmacist: When he got the bill for his malpractice insurance, he decided to go to law school.

Pharmacist: What does he mean he has a modern doctor?
Pharmacy Tech: He said he called the doctor at home and told him he was sick. The doctor told him to take two aspirin and fax him in the morning.

Pharmacist: Why do you think bank rates are high?
Pharmacy Tech: I was in the bank this morning and the loan

officer was wearing a ski mask.

Pharmacist: Why don't you like that bar?
Pharmacy Tech: They make you wear shoes and a tie to come in and watch a topless dancer.

Pharmacy Tech: My wife wants to dye her hair back to it's original color.
Pharmacist: What's stopping her?
Pharmacy Tech: She can't remember what it was.

Pharmacy Tech: The shortstop caught a line drive on the fly.
Pharmacist: What happened?
Pharmacy Tech: It ruined his sex life.

Pharmacist: Why don't you like your barber?
Pharmacy Tech: He talks behind my back.

Pharmacist: Why don't you like the new bank?
Pharmacy Tech: Because the guy who writes the ads is not the one who makes the loans!

Pharmacy Tech: He said the dentist wanted $50 to extract his tooth. He told the dentist that was too much for 20 seconds' work.
Pharmacist: What did the dentist say?
Pharmacy Tech: He said he could pull it real slow.

Pharmacy Tech: What's the best way to get a doctor to make a house call?
Pharmacist: Marry one.

Pharmacy Tech: The doctor asked him if he was taking his medicine regularly.

Pharmacist: What did he tell the doctor?
Pharmacy Tech: He told him he tasted it and decided to keep on coughing.

Pharmacy Tech: How's business?
Pharmacist: Business is so bad that even the shoplifters have stopped coming in.

Pharmacist: Our accountant opened a branch office but it didn't work out.
Pharmacy Tech: What happened?
Pharmacist: Nobody wanted to buy branches.

Pharmacy Tech: My son is studying to be a bone specialist.
Pharmacist: He certainly has the head for it.

Pharmacy Tech: What will your son be when he graduates?
Pharmacist: An old man.

Pharmacist: What kind of an insurance policy did you buy?
Pharmacy Tech: I bought a retirement policy. I pay the premium for 20 years and the salesman can retire.

Pharmacist: How is your insurance policy?
Pharmacy Tech: The big print giveth. The small print taketh away.

Pharmacist: What happened to that fellow who sent you flowers every week?
Pharmacy Tech: He married the girl who sold the flowers.

Pharmacist: Do you know anything about the bears and the bulls?

Pharmacy Tech: No, but I know all about the birds and the bees.

Pharmacist: I understand your son is a writer. Does he write for money?
Pharmacy Tech: He sure does, in every letter we get.

Pharmacy Tech: My wife wanted to see the world.
Pharmacist: What did you do?
Pharmacy Tech: I bought her an atlas.

Pharmacist: How's your wife's driving?
Pharmacy Tech: She's been stopped so often they finally gave her a season ticket.

Pharmacy Tech: What is a comedian?
Pharmacist: He's a guy who knows a good joke when he steals it.

Pharmacist: Do you like my humor?
Pharmacy Tech: You have some funny lines. It's too bad they're all in your face.

Pharmacist: How small is your home town?
Pharmacy Tech: They had to fire the dog catcher. They caught the dog.

Pharmacist: Why do you say you have a very practical doctor?
Pharmacy Tech: If you can't afford the operation he will touch up your x-rays.

Pharmacist: How was the weather in Florida?
Pharmacy Tech: It was so cold they were selling frozen

orange juice off the trees.

Pharmacist: What's so bad about a small town?
Pharmacy Tech: Once you've seen the cannon in the park there's nothing to do.

Pharmacy Tech: What is a truthful woman?
Pharmacist: One who won't lie about anything but her age, her weight and her husband's salary.

Pharmacy Tech: Which would you rather give up, wine or women?
Pharmacist: It depends on the vintage.

Pharmacist: Is your wife outspoken?
Pharmacy Tech: Not by anyone I know of.

Pharmacist: Why are you always late?
Pharmacy Tech: Every time I ask someone what time it is I get a different answer.

Pharmacy Tech: How can you tell that a man is getting along in years?
Pharmacist: When he pays more attention to the food than the waitress.

Pharmacist: What kind of time did you have in California?
Pharmacy Tech: Pacific Standard Time.

Pharmacy Tech: How can I get rid of a headache?
Pharmacist: Stick your head through the window and the pane will disappear.

Pharmacist: Why do you say it's an expensive restaurant?
Pharmacy Tech: Because you need a cosigner for a ham sandwich.

Pharmacist: How do you know that it is an authentic Mexican restaurant?
Pharmacy Tech: Because you're not supposed to drink the water.

Pharmacy Tech: The food in that restaurant was so bad that I asked to see the manager.
Pharmacist: What did he say?
Pharmacy Tech: I didn't see him, he was out to lunch.

Pharmacist: Is your son a good student?
Pharmacy Tech: The only thing he passed in college was a football.

Pharmacist: If you take out that insurance policy on your husband and he dies tomorrow, how much will you get?
Pharmacy Tech: Twenty years.

Pharmacist: What's keeping you out of the stock market?
Pharmacy Tech: The supermarket.

Pharmacy Tech: I got a necktie for my husband.
Pharmacist: You made a good trade.

Pharmacist: Who's the lady with the little wart?
Pharmacy Tech: Not so loud, that's her husband.

Pharmacist: Do you have hot and cold water at your apartment?
Pharmacy Tech: Yes. It's hot in the summer and cold in the winter.

Pharmacist: How much are they asking for your rent now?
Pharmacy Tech: About twice a week.

Pharmacy Tech: He gave me three days to pay my rent.
Pharmacist: What did you do?
Pharmacy Tech: I picked Christmas, New Years and the Fourth of July.

Pharmacist: Do they change the sheets every day?
Pharmacy Tech: Yes, from one bed to another.

Pharmacy Tech: I'm seeking your daughter's hand.
Pharmacist: You'll find it in my pocket.

Pharmacy Tech: I never repeat gossip.
Pharmacist: Good, I'll listen close the first time.

Pharmacist: You certainly look like Helen Green.
Pharmacy Tech: I look worse in pink.

Pharmacy Tech: Why did you buy me such a small diamond?
Pharmacist: I didn't want the glare to hurt your eyes.

Pharmacy Tech: What did you get your wife for her birthday?
Pharmacist: I gave her a gift certificate and she exchanged it.

Pharmacy Tech: What can I give to a man who has everything?
Pharmacist: A burglar alarm.

Pharmacy Tech: Thirty is a nice age for a woman.
Pharmacist: Especially if she happens to be 40.

Pharmacy Tech: She said the doctor told her she had a split personality.
Pharmacist: What happened?
Pharmacy Tech: He charged her for two office calls.

Pharmacy Tech: He said the psychiatrist told him he was completely cured and there was no need for further appointments.
Pharmacist: Then why is the patient mad at the psychiatrist?
Pharmacy Tech: He said two years ago he was Napoleon and today he is nobody!

Pharmacy Tech: She told the doctor she feels a strange man is following her wherever she goes.
Pharmacist: What did the doctor tell her?
Pharmacy Tech: The doctor told her the man is from the collection agency and he is trying to collect the doctor's bill.

Pharmacy Tech: The patient said the psychiatrist has been treating him for kleptomania and the doctor told him he thinks he is completely cured.
Pharmacist: Then why is the patient so unhappy?
Pharmacy Tech: The doctor told him if he has a relapse he could use a portable computer.

Pharmacy Tech: My doctor told me to take a bath before

retiring.

Pharmacist: At your age you won't be able to retire for 30 years.

Pharmacist: You've got a terrible haircut.
Pharmacy Tech: My barber gives a lousy hair cut but he has some great stories.

Pharmacist: What did he say about his past due account?
Pharmacy Tech: He said he couldn't pay it. But if you would take him down in the basement he would show you how to fix your meter so you can cheat the gas company.

Pharmacist: What did she say when you asked her if she had difficulty making up her mind?
Pharmacy Tech: She said yes and no.

Pharmacy Tech: He said the doctor asked him if he could pay for an operation if he needed one.
Pharmacist: What did he tell the doctor?
Pharmacy Tech: He asked the doctor if he would need the operation if he couldn't pay for it.

Pharmacy Tech: He said he is 91 years old and still chases women.
Pharmacist: What's wrong with that?
Pharmacy Tech: He can't remember why he's chasing them.

Pharmacy Tech: He said he told the bartender he wanted something tall and cold and full of gin.
Pharmacist: What did the bartender say?
Pharmacy Tech: He said the bartender told him to wait a minute and he would go and get his wife.

Pharmacy Tech: What's the best way to stay young?
Pharmacist: Hang out with older people.

Pharmacy Tech: If you could choose your way to die, how would it be?
Pharmacist : From smoke inhalation from blowing out the candles on my 100th birthday cake.

Pharmacy Tech: He said he has the five B's of old age.
Pharmacist: Did he say what that is?
Pharmacy Tech: Bunions, bifocals, balding, bulges and bursitis.

Pharmacist: We're having my new son christened this Sunday.
Pharmacy Tech: He seems awful small to have a bottle smashed over his head.

Pharmacy Tech: Why don't blind people skydive?
Pharmacist: Because it scares the heck out of their seeing-eye dogs.

Pharmacy Tech: What did the flasher say to the woman in subzero weather?
Pharmacist: It's so cold — should I just describe myself?

Pharmacy Tech: How do you know when you're getting older?
Pharmacist: There are 12 candles on your piece of birthday cake.

Pharmacy Tech: Why didn't she pass her Pharmacy State Board examination?

Pharmacist: She couldn't get the little bottles into the typewriter.

Pharmacy Tech: He wants to know how to get to Carnegie Hall.
Pharmacist: Tell him there are three things he has to do: practice, practice, practice.

Pharmacist: Did the movie have a happy ending?
Pharmacy Tech: Yes, everyone was glad it was over.

Pharmacy Tech: How did you enjoy the banquet speaker?
Pharmacist: It amazed me how he could eat so much chicken and ham and be so full of bull.

Pharmacy Tech: What's the difference between a Southern Baptist and a Northern Baptist?
Pharmacist: A Southern Baptist says, "There ain't no hell!" and a Northern Baptist says, "The hell there ain't."

Pharmacy Tech: What do you mean they separated because of religious differences?
Pharmacist: He's a pharmacist, she's a Christian Scientist.

Pharmacist: Do you partake of intoxicating beverages?
Pharmacy Tech: Is that an inquiry or an invitation?

Pharmacy Tech: She's a beautiful girl.
Pharmacist: She got her good looks from her father—he's a plastic surgeon.

Pharmacy Tech: How can you tell if an Italian is in the Mafia?
Pharmacist: His favorite dish is broken leg of lamb.

Pharmacist: Why did they name the baby Seven and Three Eighths?
Pharmacy Tech: His mother picked his name out of a hat.

Pharmacy Tech: The waiter said either a white wine or a light red wine would be appropriate with our entree.
Pharmacist: Which did you order?
Pharmacy Tech: I told him to bring either one, I'm color blind.

Pharmacy Tech: The teacher sent a note home saying my son should have the use of an encyclopedia.
Pharmacist: What did you tell the teacher?
Pharmacy Tech: I told the teacher that I had to walk to school when I was a kid and my son could do the same.

Pharmacy Tech: I've got a very funny Polish joke to tell you.
Pharmacist: Now remember, I'm Polish.
Pharmacy Tech: OK, I'll tell it very SLOWLY.

Pharmacy Tech: Why do you play so much golf?
Pharmacist: Because my doctor told me I must take my iron every day.

Pharmacist: Why do you think that salesman is a smart cookie?
Pharmacy Tech: He thinks twice before saying nothing.

Pharmacy Tech: How do you get a pharmacist out of a tree?
Pharmacist: I have no idea. How do you do that?
Pharmacy Tech: Wave at him.

Pharmacy Tech: What's the definition of a faithful husband?

Pharmacist: That's a husband whose alimony checks never bounce.

Pharmacy Tech: How can you tell when a woman's cooking is really lousy?
Pharmacist: Natives come from the Amazon to dip their arrows in it.

Pharmacy Tech: What's the difference between a drunk and an alcoholic?
Pharmacist: A drunk doesn't have to go to all those meetings.

Pharmacy Tech: What is the penalty for bigamy?
Pharmacist: You get two mothers-in-law.

Pharmacy Tech: What is the difference between a pessimist and an optimist?
Pharmacist: A pessimist is a fellow who really knows what's going on. An optimist is a fellow who hasn't read the morning papers.

Pharmacist: Why do you think this company lacks an open mind?
Pharmacy Tech: The suggestion box is a garbage disposal.

Pharmacy Tech: Why do you say your stockbroker is a professional consultant?
Pharmacist: He knows 50 ways to make love and can't get a girl.

Pharmacy Tech: How would you define the term stockbroker?
Pharmacist: A stockbroker is a person who rides to work on

the city bus and tells people who drive to work in a BMW
how to invest their money.

Pharmacy Tech: Are women smarter than men?
Pharmacist: Diamonds are a girl's best friend and dogs are
a man's best friend. You figure it out for yourself.

Pharmacy Tech: What should I look for in a man?
Pharmacist: Look for an older man with a strong will—
made out to you.

Pharmacy Tech: If a girl breaks her engagement, should she
return the ring?
Pharmacist: The proper thing to do is return the ring—but
she should keep the diamond.

Pharmacy Tech: My brother-in-law just opened a pharmacy.
Pharmacist: How is he doing?
Pharmacy Tech: Not very well. It wasn't his pharmacy.

Pharmacy Tech: What did the sign on your stockbroker's
desk say?
Pharmacist: It said, "The buck drops here."

Pharmacy Tech: Why do you say a woman will never be
elected president?
Pharmacist: They never reach the legal age to run.

Pharmacist: Why did you join the women's lib movement?
Pharmacy Tech: I want to get married and not have to work
any more.

Pharmacy Tech: Why do you say he's a good drug rep?
Pharmacist: He can yawn with his mouth closed.

Pharmacy Tech: How can you tell a smart drug salesman?
Pharmacist: He never stands between a dog and a hydrant.

Pharmacist: Why did the doctor have you go to the window and stick out your tongue?
Pharmacy Tech: He was mad at his neighbor.

Pharmacy Tech: What happened to your stockbroker?
Pharmacist: He was wrong so many times he got a job as a government economist.

Pharmacist: Why do you say your vacation to Mexico reminded you of Eve's experience in the Garden of Eden?
Pharmacy Tech: All of my troubles started when I bit into a piece of fruit.

Pharmacist: Where are you going for your vacation this year?
Pharmacy Tech: To the usual place, the bank for a loan.

Pharmacy Tech: What is a diplomatic drug rep?
Pharmacist: One who can tell you to go to hell in such a way that you actually enjoy the trip.

Pharmacy Tech: What did the sign in the obstetrician's office say?
Pharmacist: The sign said, "WE DELIVER 24 HOURS A DAY."

Pharmacy Tech: Why won't the battle of the sexes ever be won?
Pharmacist: There's too much fraternizing with the enemy.

Pharmacist: Did you come from a small town?

Pharmacy Tech: Our 24-hour diner closed at noon.

Pharmacy Tech: Why do you think we have such a clean city?
Pharmacist: The taxpayers get taken to the cleaners every day.

Pharmacist: Will you love your wife when she's old and wrinkled?
Pharmacy Tech: Of course I do.

Pharmacist: What do you mean the doctor made you a deal?
Pharmacy Tech: He'll take out my appendix if I take out his daughter.

Pharmacist: Why do you say your husband is not very handsome?
Pharmacy Tech: Customs made him put someone else's picture on his passport.

Pharmacy Tech: What do you think would be the best way to solve the early morning traffic problem?
Pharmacist: Keep all the cars that aren't paid for off the freeway until noon.

Pharmacy Tech: How did he get to be the richest man in town?
Pharmacist: He's a plumber who moonlights as a television repairman.

Pharmacy Tech: What's the best way to save money on long distance phone calls?
Pharmacist: Wait for your friends to call you.

Pharmacy Tech: What did that TV commercial say four out of five pharmacists prefer?
Pharmacist: What four out of five pharmacists prefer can't be shown on TV.

Pharmacy Tech: How can that phone company offer a toll free 800 number for a dollar a month?
Pharmacist: Customers can call from anywhere, 24 hours a day, toll free, and get a busy signal.

Pharmacy Tech: Why do you say that salesman is an honest man?
Pharmacist: When he does his 1040 tax return, he reports half of his salary as unearned income.

Pharmacy Tech: Why do you say your lawyer is so dependable?
Pharmacist: He's available twenty-four hours a day. All I have to do is call, and the warden brings him to the phone.

Pharmacy Tech: How does that Cigarette Anonymous work?
Pharmacist: When you feel like smoking you dial an 800 number and you hear a minute of coughing.

Pharmacy Tech: Did you say you lied on your income tax return last year?
Pharmacist: Yes. I listed myself as head of the household.

Pharmacy Tech: Does the IRS have an easy payment plan?
Pharmacist: Yes, 100 percent down and nothing per month.

Pharmacist: There is a certain amount of pride to being an American taxpayer.
Pharmacy Tech: I could be just as proud for half the price.

Pharmacy Tech: I asked my minister if it is a sin to play golf on Sunday.
Pharmacist: What did your minister say?
Pharmacy Tech: He said the way I play, it is a sin to play any day.

Pharmacist: What did that salesman say were the two happiest days of his life?
Pharmacy Tech: The day he bought a boat and the day he sold it.

Pharmacist: Why do you say you came from a very small town?
Pharmacy Tech: When we had a Fourth of July parade, there was no one to watch it. Everybody in town was in the parade.

Pharmacy Tech: What's the best way to stop smoking?
Pharmacist: Use wet matches.

Pharmacy Tech: What did the sign in the empty drug store building say?
Pharmacist: It said, "See, I told you we had the lowest prices in town."

Pharmacist: How small was your home town?
Pharmacy Tech: We only had one fire hydrant and the fire department kept a dog to help them find it.

Pharmacy Tech: Why do you say today is going to be a tough day?
Pharmacist: The computer broke down and we're going to have to think for ourselves.

Pharmacy Tech: Do you find that salesman boring?
Pharmacist: The room lights up when he leaves.

Pharmacist: How come you never get a parking ticket?
Pharmacy Tech: I removed my windshield wipers.

Pharmacist: Is your wife a good cook?
Pharmacy Tech: She made toast every day until she lost the recipe.

Pharmacy Tech: Would you like to buy a ticket for a Catholic benefit?
Pharmacist: I never refuse to buy a ticket for any religious benefit. I did once and it snowed in my living room for five days.

Pharmacist: What did that senior citizen tell you?
Pharmacy Tech: I gave him his umbrella and he said we were the only honest merchants in town. All the others denied having it.

Pharmacist: My wife has a very bad memory.
Pharmacy Tech: You mean she forgets everything?
Pharmacist: No, she remembers everything.

Pharmacy Tech: What do you think of the direction pharmacy is taking?
Pharmacist: I think it is just great. I can see a whole new field of unemployment opening up.

Pharmacy Tech: How many prescriptions does the average pharmacist fill?
Pharmacist: There are three answers to your question. The number he would like to fill, the number he actually fills

and the number he tells the pharmaceutical salesmen that he fills.

Pharmacist: My wife said I am married to the drug store and I should sell it, but I told her I couldn't do that.
Pharmacy Tech: What did she say?
Pharmacist: She said then I should sue it for non-support.

Pharmacy Tech: My wife said all of her weight was just water.
Pharmacist: What did you tell her?
Pharmacy Tech: I told her that was very true. On the right side she's got the Atlantic Ocean, on the left, the Pacific, and in the rear, the Dead Sea.

Pharmacist: Pharmacists were the originators of the expression, "blood, sweat and tears."
Pharmacy Tech: What do you mean by that?
Pharmacist: They give blood to the blood bank. They sweat trying to make a buck. Then, they shed tears when they have a slow day.

Pharmacist: How did the wedding go?
Pharmacy Tech: The bride was so homely that everyone kissed the bridesmaid.

Pharmacy Tech: Why do you say advertising is very effective?
Pharmacist: Before all the advertising, a virus was known as the flu.

Pharmacy Tech: What did you think of that salesman?
Pharmacist: He has nothing to say, but you have to listen to him a long time to find that out.

Pharmacy Tech: What do you spread over your strawberries?
Pharmacist: Manure.
Pharmacy Tech: You ought to come over to our place; we use whipped cream.

Pharmacy Tech: This company seems to be like one big, happy family.
Pharmacist: That's because I have to hire so many of my wife's relatives.

Pharmacy Tech: How was her résumé?
Pharmacist: It was very impressive, especially the centerfold.

Pharmacy Tech: Why do you only pay us once a month?
Pharmacist: Because you can't buy anything with a week's salary.

Pharmacist: What did the father of your bride tell you?
Pharmacy Tech: He said I was the second happiest man in the world.

Pharmacy Tech: What's wrong with owning a pharmacy?
Pharmacist: If you do something wrong, you're fined; if you do something right, you're taxed.

Pharmacy Tech: What's the best way to find out how to run a pharmacy?
Pharmacist: Ask a pharmacist who doesn't own one.

Pharmacy Tech: I regret the day I told her about my rich uncle.
Pharmacist: What happened?

Pharmacy Tech: She became my rich aunt.

Pharmacy Tech: She said she had something that would knock my eyes out.
Pharmacist: What did she have?
Pharmacy Tech: A husband.

Pharmacy Tech: I told her I wanted some old fashion loving.
Pharmacist: What did she tell you?
Pharmacy Tech: She said she would introduce me to her grandmother.

Pharmacy Tech: Don't hire him, he's no good. He will lie, cheat and steal. He will do anything to make a buck.
Pharmacist: How do you know that?
Pharmacy Tech: He used to work for me and I taught him everything he knows.

Pharmacy Tech: What did the cannibal give his wife for a Valentine's Day gift?
Pharmacist: I don't know, what did he give her?
Pharmacy Tech: A five-pound box of farmers' fannies.

Pharmacist: We've been in Rome for five days and I haven't been to the Colosseum yet.
Pharmacy Tech: Neither have I, that's why I took a laxative this morning.

Pharmacy Tech: That salesman said his district manager questioned him on his expense account. He asked him how he could spend $25 a day on food in Sioux Falls.
Pharmacist: What did he tell his sales manager?
Pharmacy Tech: He told him it's very simple to do, just go without breakfast.

Pharmacy Tech: The man on the phone said he can't ship our order until you pay for the last one.
Pharmacist: Tell him to cancel the order, we can't wait that long.

Pharmacy Tech: Why don't you take your wife along when you go to the convention?
Pharmacist: If I take my wife along, I have twice the expense and half the fun.

Pharmacy Tech: On the salary you pay me I can't afford to get married.
Pharmacist: That's right, and in 20 years you'll be thanking me.

Pharmacy Tech: How do you know he's a hypochondriac?
Pharmacist: Because he can read his doctor's handwriting.

Pharmacist: Money can't buy happiness.
Pharmacy Tech: No, but it can make a big dent in the down payment.

Pharmacy Tech: How do you get your exercise?
Pharmacist: I get my exercise by being a pall bearer at the funerals of my friends who exercise.

Pharmacy Tech: Why do you think he is a good manager?
Pharmacist: He never puts off until tomorrow what he can get you to do today.

Pharmacist: Do you have a happy marriage?
Pharmacy Tech: For 20 years my husband and I were very happy—then we met.

Pharmacy Tech: I told my wife that you said money can't
buy happiness.
Pharmacist: What did she say to that?
Pharmacy Tech: She said you didn't know where to shop.

Pharmacist: What does he mean he wants to shop at a
friendly pharmacy?
Pharmacy Tech: He says that's one that not only delivers
but they arrange financing.

Pharmacy Tech: What is the most common cause of car
sickness?
Pharmacist: The sticker price on the window.

Pharmacist: Why don't you try to pay as you go?
Pharmacy Tech: Because I have to pay for where I've
already been.

Pharmacist: I think you're a good egg.
Pharmacy Tech: Thanks, but I happen to know where eggs
come from.

Pharmacist: That salesman is a real magician.
Pharmacy Tech: What do you mean by that?
Pharmacist: He can make an ass out of himself.

Pharmacy Tech: What did you tell that salesman?
Pharmacist: I told him that I never forget a face, but in his
case I would make an exception.

Pharmacy Tech: When I was sixteen, I was chosen Miss
South Dakota.
Pharmacist: In those days there were very few people in
South Dakota.

Pharmacy Tech: Is he a good salesman?
Pharmacist: The only orders he takes are from his wife.

Pharmacist: Did insurance take care of your hospital bill?
Pharmacy Tech: No, I have a group policy. The whole group has to get sick before I can collect.

Pharmacist: Did you see the sign at the Las Vegas dice table?
Pharmacy Tech: No, what did it say?
Pharmacist: It said: SHAKE WELL BEFORE LOSING.

Pharmacist: What did your insurance agent say?
Pharmacy Tech: He said honesty is the best policy, except when you're trying to collect on this policy.

Pharmacy Tech: Does this job have any death benefits?
Pharmacist: If you die, you don't have to come to work.

Pharmacy Tech: He said he went into a drug store in Las Vegas to get some aspirin. The clerk said, "I'll toss you for it, double or nothing,"
Pharmacist: What happened?
Pharmacy Tech: He ended up with two headaches.

Pharmacist: How much did you pay for that toupee?
Pharmacy Tech: It cost me $1,200.
Pharmacist: Good grief, even Jesse James didn't have that kind of a price on his head.

Pharmacist: What did you get when you hung your stocking last Christmas?
Pharmacy Tech: A note from the health department.

Pharmacy Tech: My wife said if it wasn't for her money our furniture wouldn't be here.
Pharmacist: What did you tell her?
Pharmacy Tech: I told her that if it wasn't for her money, I wouldn't be here.

Pharmacist: What did you get your mother for Mother's Day?
Pharmacy Tech: I got her a new washer/dryer.
Pharmacist: What did she do with her old one?
Pharmacy Tech: She divorced him last year.

Pharmacist: Did you say you left your wife because of another woman?
Pharmacy Tech: Yes, her mother.

Pharmacist: Why do you always give your wife money for her birthday?
Pharmacy Tech: So she can't take it back and exchange it for something bigger.

Pharmacy Tech: Why do you say that drug clerk is honest?
Pharmacist: This morning she called in lazy.

Pharmacist: Religion is making a comeback in this country.
Pharmacy Tech: Why do you say that?
Pharmacist: Sixty percent of all Americans are going to church and the other 40 percent are putting their faith in the lottery.

Pharmacy Tech: Why do you wear two pair of pants when you play golf?
Pharmacist: In case I get a hole in one.

Pharmacy Tech: Why do you say Adam and Eve had a peaceful marriage?

Pharmacist: Because he never bragged about his mother's cooking, and she never talked about the other men she could have married.

Pharmacy Tech: I read some bad news today.

Pharmacist: What did you read?

Pharmacy Tech: The cost of living has gone up $2 a quart.

Pharmacy Tech: He said he told the doctor he had been leading a normal life.

Pharmacist: What did the doctor say?

Pharmacy Tech: The doctor told him to cut it out for a while.

Pharmacy Tech: She said the doctor agreed to make a house call.

Pharmacist: How did that happen?

Pharmacy Tech: The doctor told her he had another patient in the same area and he would kill two birds with one stone.

Pharmacy Tech: What did the doctor prescribe for her sick husband?

Pharmacist: He prescribed sleeping pills and told her to take them.

Pharmacy Tech: Did he tell the doctor why he couldn't pay his bill?

Pharmacist: Yes, he told the doctor that he slowed down like he told him to and he lost his job.

Pharmacy Tech: He said the psychiatrist asked him how long he had the feeling that he was a dog.

216

Pharmacist: What did he tell the doctor?
Pharmacy Tech: He said, "Ever since I was a puppy."

Pharmacist: Did he say that they x-rayed his wife's jaw?
Pharmacy Tech: He said they tried to but they ended up with a moving picture.

Pharmacist: When you go, how would you like to go?
Pharmacy Tech: When I go, I want to go peacefully, in my sleep, like my grandfather, not screaming in terror like his passengers.

Pharmacist: Did I hear you had an auto accident on the way to work this morning?
Pharmacy Tech: Yes, I ran into the back of a car at that stop sign on 5th Street. I don't know why people don't watch where they're going, that's the fourth accident I've had this week.

Pharmacy Tech: They say it's lonely at the top.
Pharmacist: That may be, but you eat better up there.

Pharmacy Tech: How do you know that water attracts electricity?
Pharmacist: Because the phone always rings when I'm in the shower.

Pharmacist: How was your class reunion?
Pharmacy Tech: Everyone got so old they didn't recognize me.

Pharmacy Tech: How did your physical examination go?
Pharmacist: The doctor told me to give up wine and women but I could still sing.

217

Pharmacy Tech: Did you put all your eggs in one basket?
Pharmacist: Yes, but I'm watching the basket.

Pharmacy Tech: Do old psychiatrists ever die?
Pharmacist: No, they just SHRINK away.

Pharmacy Tech: What words of wisdom do you have for me today?
Pharmacist: Never accept a drink from a urologist.

Pharmacy Tech: Why does that doctor favor breast-feeding?
Pharmacist: He says the milk is always at the right temperature, it comes in attractive containers, and the cat can't get at it.

Pharmacy Tech: What did you think of jury duty?
Pharmacist: It's 12 people deciding who has the best lawyer.

Pharmacy Tech: What's the best way to lose weight?
Pharmacist: Just eat all you want of everything you don't like.

Pharmacist: How long do you intend to keep this job?
Pharmacy Tech: From here to maternity.

Pharmacy Tech: Just how old are you?
Pharmacist: When I was your age, they called the flag Young Glory.

Pharmacy Tech: Was it crowded at the night club last night?
Pharmacist: Not under my table.

Pharmacist: I got a TV set for my husband.
Pharmacy Tech: I wish I could make a trade like that.

Pharmacy Tech: How can I avoid falling hair?
Pharmacist: Jump out of its way.

Pharmacy Tech: What did the fountain girl say when you told her the coffee was weak?
Pharmacist: She said that ain't the coffee, it's the soup.

Pharmacy Tech: Should a woman have children after 35?
Pharmacist: No, 35 children are enough.

Pharmacy Tech: What did the waitress say when you told her you were so hungry you could eat a horse?
Pharmacist: She said I couldn't have come to a better place.

Pharmacy Tech: Money can't buy happiness.
Pharmacist: No, but it lets you get a bigger shopping bag.

Pharmacist: Are you happy in your job?
Pharmacy Tech: I never knew what real happiness was until I started working here; but then, it was too late.

Pharmacist: Are you still trying to keep up with the Joneses?
Pharmacy Tech: No, I've decided to drag them down to my level.

Pharmacist: Are you on a diet?
Pharmacy Tech: If my wife's on a diet, everyone's on a diet.

Pharmacist: Why aren't you working?
Pharmacy Tech: Because I didn't hear you coming.

Pharmacist: What do you get when you cross a lawyer with a godfather?
Pharmacy Tech: An offer you can't understand.

Pharmacist: How can you tell if I have been using the computer?
Pharmacy Tech: There's white-out on the screen.

Pharmacist: Why are you late again?
Pharmacy Tech: It makes the day shorter.

Pharmacy Tech: I think I made a goof!
Pharmacist: To err is human but to really foul up requires a computer.

Pharmacist: You should have been here at nine o'clock!
Pharmacy Tech: Why, what happened?

Pharmacy Tech: You say you made a killing in the stock market?
Pharmacist: Yes, I shot my broker.

Pharmacy Tech: I'd like to talk to you about a raise.

220

I've been praying for one in church every Sunday.
Pharmacist: What did I tell you about going over my head?

Pharmacy Tech: What are the rewards of working at this job?
Pharmacist: If you work faithfully for eight hours a day, you may eventually become boss and then you can work twelve hours a day.

Pharmacist: You're late again, do you have any idea what time we start working here?
Pharmacy Tech: I have no idea, everyone is always working by the time I get here.

Pharmacy Tech: Someone on the phone wants to know how many employees we have, broken down by sex.
Pharmacist: Tell him alcoholism is more of a problem here.

Pharmacy Tech: My son opened a submarine shop.
Pharmacist: How did it go?
Pharmacy Tech: He went under.

Pharmacist: What do you get when you play a country song backwards?
Pharmacy Tech: You get your wife back, you get your job back, and you stop drinking.

Pharmacist: What do you mean when you say, "Last night you slept like an attorney?"
Pharmacy Tech: First I'd lie on one side, then I'd lie on the other.

Pharmacist: What's the best thing to throw to a drown-

ing guitar player?
Pharmacy Tech: His amplifier.

Pharmacist: What is the definition of a gentleman?
Pharmacy Tech: Someone who can play the accordion and won't.

Pharmacy Tech: How does a pharmacist make a million dollars?
Pharmacist: He starts out with five million.

Pharmacy Tech: What part of the car causes the most accidents?
Pharmacist: The nut behind the wheel.

Pharmacy Tech: He said the doctor told him his check came back.
Pharmacist: What did he tell the doctor?
Pharmacy Tech: So did my arthritis.

Pharmacy Tech: He said he had a dime stuck in his ear for a year.
Pharmacist: Why didn't he see the doctor sooner?
Pharmacy Tech: He didn't need the money.

Pharmacy Tech: She said she asked the doctor if she could get a second opinion.
Pharmacist: What did the doctor say?
Pharmacy Tech: The doctor said certainly, come back tomorrow.

Pharmacy Tech: She told the doctor she had a ringing in her ears.
Pharmacist: What did the doctor say?
Pharmacy Tech: He told her not to answer it.

Pharmacist: What makes you think you have such a fancy doctor?
Pharmacy Tech: You have to make an appointment to make an appointment.

Pharmacy Tech: You fired the janitor, when are you going to fill the vacancy?
Pharmacist: He didn't leave any.

Pharmacy Tech: Does she give you an honest day's work?
Pharmacist: Yes, but it takes her a week to do it.

Pharmacist: Why do you think you should have an extra day's vacation?
Pharmacy Tech: To make up for all the coffee breaks I missed on vacation.

Pharmacist: What do you mean that doctor is mean but fair?
Pharmacy Tech: He's mean to everyone.

Pharmacist: Did you pass your chemistry lab test?
Pharmacy Tech: I don't know. The teacher hasn't come down yet.

Pharmacist: There will be an eclipse of the moon at 10 p.m. Be sure to watch it.
Pharmacy Tech: What channel is it on?

Pharmacist: Do you understand what an atom is?
Pharmacy Tech: Wasn't he the guy who was the husband of Eve?

Pharmacist: Last week I overpaid you and you didn't say anything. This week I adjusted my error and you complained. How come?

Pharmacy Tech: I can overlook one error, but two in a row is too much.

Pharmacist: What do you call a tourniquet worn on the left hand that stops circulation?
Pharmacy Tech: A wedding ring.

Pharmacy Tech: Money isn't everything.
Pharmacist: No, but it sure does keep you in touch with your children.

Pharmacist: What have you learned about child care?
Pharmacy Tech: Never change diapers in mid-stream.

Pharmacist: Boys will be boys.
Pharmacy Tech: So will a lot of middle-age men.

Pharmacy Tech: Is your mother-in-law still visiting your house?
Pharmacist: I dropped her off at the airport this morning. She leaves tomorrow.

Pharmacist: How's the new baby doing?
Pharmacy Tech: People who say they sleep like a baby usually don't have one.

Pharmacist: How do your children brighten your home?
Pharmacy Tech: They forget to turn out the lights.

Pharmacist: What is the name of your bank?
Pharmacy Tech: Piggy.

Pharmacist: Lend me a dime. I want to call a friend.
Pharmacy Tech: Here are two. Call both of them.

Pharmacist: How did you find the steak?
Pharmacy Tech: With a magnifying glass.

Pharmacist: Why did you hit your wife with a chair?
Pharmacy Tech: I couldn't lift the table.

Pharmacy Tech: My father was a Pole.
Pharmacist: North or South?

Pharmacy Tech: Every time I drink hot tea, I get a sharp pain in my left eye.
Pharmacist: Take the spoon out of your cup.

Pharmacist: How about a little gin rummy?
Pharmacy Tech: No thanks, I never touch the stuff.

Pharmacist: Has the doctor you're engaged to got any money?
Pharmacy Tech: He sure has. Do you think I'm getting married for my health?

Pharmacy Tech: The customer said he has a virus.
Pharmacist: That's what everybody gets when they can't spell pneumonia.

Pharmacy Tech: What's a cold tablet?
Pharmacist: That's what an Eskimo writes on.

Pharmacist: What did he say about sex?
Pharmacy Tech: He said that's what they put

potatoes in when he lived in North Dakota.

Pharmacist: What would you get if you crossed a germ with a comedian?
Pharmacy Tech: A sick joke.

Pharmacy Tech: I want a raise or count me out.
Pharmacist: One, two, three, four, five, six, seven, eight, nine, ten.

Pharmacist: Congratulations!
Pharmacy Tech: For what?
Pharmacist: This is the earliest that you have been late.

Pharmacist: Don't discuss salary with others, it's personal business.
Pharmacy Tech: Don't worry. I'm as ashamed of it as you are.

Pharmacy Tech: She said she feels like herself again.
Pharmacist: In that case she needs more treatment.

Pharmacy Tech: She wants to know if she is over-weight:
Pharmacist: Tell her no, according to the weight chart she's five inches too short.

Pharmacy Tech: Was it rheumatism?
Pharmacist: No, his suspenders were twisted.

Pharmacy Tech: Why did he have a local anesthetic?
Pharmacist: He's the Chamber of Commerce Secretary and he wanted to support a local industry.

Pharmacy Tech: How does that garlic diet work?

Pharmacist: You don't lose weight but you look thinner from a distance.

Pharmacy Tech: I finally found a way to get money out of my husband.
Pharmacist: How did you do that?
Pharmacy Tech: I told him I was going home to mother. He gave me the fare.

Pharmacy Tech: My wife and I argue and fight a lot. The least little thing sets her off.
Pharmacist: You're lucky. Mine is a self starter.

Pharmacist: Is he an old flame?
Pharmacy Tech: More like an unlit match.

Pharmacy Tech: I asked the computer to find me the perfect mate. I want a companion who is small and cute, loves water sports, and enjoys group activities.
Pharmacist: How did the computer respond?
Pharmacy Tech: It told me to marry a penguin!

Pharmacist: What happened to that dizzy blonde you used to date?
Pharmacy Tech: She dyed her hair.

Pharmacy Tech: Why did the nose-drop salesman get fired?
Pharmacist: He was sticking his business in other people's noses.

Pharmacy Tech: He said that ointment is making his leg smart.
Pharmacist: Tell him to rub some on his head.

Pharmacy Tech: She said her husband was run over

by a steam roller.
Pharmacist: Tell her to have him stay flat on his back.

Pharmacist: How did you get to be "King of the Road?"
Pharmacy Tech: My license plate says PMS. Nobody cuts me off.

Pharmacist: Why did you pay so much for a bird feeder.
Pharmacy Tech: It saved me money on cat food.

Pharmacy Tech: I told that customer that our motto is, "We Aim to Please."
Pharmacist: What did she say?
Pharmacy Tech: She said I should take some time off for target practice.

Pharmacy Tech: What do you consider a super salesman?
Pharmacist: He's a salesman who can sell a double-breasted suit to a man with a Phi Beta Kappa key.

Pharmacist: What's her complaint?
Pharmacy Tech: She says either she's got the flu or some of our Valentine candy had prune centers.

Pharmacist: How do you know he's a poor golfer?
Pharmacy Tech: He carries flares, a compass, and k-rations in his golf bag.

Pharmacist: How's your new car?
Pharmacy Tech: It has six cup holders and they tell me not to drink and drive.

Pharmacist: Did you and your wife have a romantic evening?
Pharmacy Tech: Yeah, we had dinner by candlelight. Then after we'd eaten, we burned the overdue electric bills.

Pharmacy Tech: They don't make American cars like they use to.
Pharmacist: They don't make Americans like they used to.

Pharmacist: We're having a new kind of sales contest.
Pharmacy Tech: How does it work?
Pharmacist: The winners get to keep their job.

Pharmacy Tech: How was your dental bill?
Pharmacist: I put my money where my mouth is.

Pharmacy Tech: My grandfather lived to be 98 and never used glasses.
Pharmacist: Lots of people drink from the bottle.

Pharmacist: What was your biggest vacation expense?
Pharmacy Tech: My wife.

Pharmacist: What can I give a man who has everything?
Pharmacy Tech: My phone number.

Pharmacist: So you and your wife are not speaking?
Pharmacy Tech: No, just shouting.

Pharmacy Tech: I heard you made a lot of money on the stock market.
Pharmacist: Yes, I bought 7-Up when it was only 6 1/2.

Pharmacy Tech: My wife took everything and left me.
Pharmacist: You're lucky. Mine didn't leave.

Pharmacist: I'll tell you a joke that will kill you.
Pharmacy Tech: Please don't! I'm too young to die.

Pharmacist: Work hard and you'll get ahead.
Pharmacy Tech: I've got a head.

Pharmacist: Do you feel like a cup of coffee:
Pharmacy Tech: Of course not; do I look like one?

Pharmacist: Why is she so happy with her new doctor?
Pharmacy Tech: He treated her for double pneumonia but only charged her for one.

Pharmacy Tech: If I take the job will I get a raise in salary every year?
Pharmacist: Yes, provided, of course, that your work is satisfactory.
Pharmacy Tech: I knew there would be a catch.

Pharmacist: Why do you think you stayed too late at the party?
Pharmacy Tech: The host was in his pajamas having an Alka-Seltzer.

Pharmacist: Is everybody sick at your house?
Pharmacy Tech: Yeah! You have to take a number just to use the vaporizer.

Pharmacy Tech: What was that bit you told me about a smile?

Pharmacist: A smile costs nothing and gives much. It takes but a moment, but the memory of it can last forever. It creates happiness in the home, fosters good will in business and is the countersign of friendship. Some people are too tired to give you a smile. Give them one of yours. None needs a smile as much as those who have no more to give.

Humor in Pharmacy

About the Author

Cliff Thomas has been a pharmacist for more than 50 years, and during that time he has filled more than a million prescriptions.

Starting as a soda jerk in the corner drug store at the age of 12, he has practiced almost every facet of the profession of pharmacy. From being the manager of a prescription department of a large super drugstore, to a professional pharmacy manager, to the owner of his own community pharmacy, to an instructor in pharmacy, a research pharmacist to a hospital pharmacist, and finally to a State Board of Pharmacy inspector. Cliff Thomas has done it all.

He has served as president of his state pharmacists association, received pharmacy's coveted Bowl of Hygeia award, and was recently named South Dakota's Pharmacist of the Year.

After retiring from retail pharmacy, Cliff became a humorous after-dinner speaker. A pharmacist talking humorously to pharmacists about pharmacy, and to anyone else who will listen.

He has given more than 500 presentations to various groups across the United States. His well-received messages have been described as motivating, versatile, funny, interesting, and entertaining.

Through the years, Cliff has collected humorous material about the profession of pharmacy, the people pharmacists serve, and their allied professionals. In addition to his vast humor library, he has three file cabinets packed with items clipped from various publications or quotes to him by other pharmacists.

"A teaspoon of sugar makes the medicine go down," and Cliff sincerely believes that laughter is the best medicine, as reflected in his books and in his presentations.

He is a natural story teller with an abundance of hilarious anecdotes from his many years as a pharmacist dealing with people.

To order additional copies of
Humor in Pharmacy . . .

PLEASE SEND ME ____ (QTY.) COPIES
Only $14.95 plus $2 shipping & handling each.
South Dakota residents please add 65 cents sales tax per book.

NAME (PLEASE PRINT) _____

ADDRESS _____

CITY/STATE/ZIP _____
Nemo Publishing Co., 1721 12th Ave., Belle Fourche, SD 57717-2112

PLEASE SEND ME ____ (QTY.) COPIES
Only $14.95 plus $2 shipping & handling each.
South Dakota residents please add 65 cents sales tax per book.

NAME (PLEASE PRINT) _____

ADDRESS _____

CITY/STATE/ZIP _____
Nemo Publishing Co., 1721 12th Ave., Belle Fourche, SD 57717-2112

PLEASE SEND ME ____ (QTY.) COPIES
Only $14.95 plus $2 shipping & handling each.
South Dakota residents please add 65 cents sales tax per book.

NAME (PLEASE PRINT) _____

ADDRESS _____

CITY/STATE/ZIP _____
Nemo Publishing Co., 1721 12th Ave., Belle Fourche, SD 57717-2112